Building Blocks

by Richard Flint, CSP

Copyright 2002

ISBN# 0-937851-29-9

*Printed in the United States of America. For information
address Flint, Inc., 11835 Canon Blvd., Suite C-105,
Newport News, VA 23606-2570
1-800-368-8255
www.richardflint.com*

Cover Design by Denise Smith
Edited by Steve Hutson

DEDICATION

*To Bill Gove whose commitment to
professional speaking and
investment of himself in my life
inspired me to reach beyond even
what I thought I could achieve as a
professional speaker.*

TABLE OF CONTENTS

The Building Blocks

Building Block #1:
Why spend your energy being a carbon copy when you are an original!

Building Block # 2:
You are perfectly designed to achieve what you are achieving.

Building Block # 3:
If what you say you want is contradicted by what you do, then you are lying to yourself and all you have said it to.

Building Block # 4:
Don't tell me what you want if you are not willing to pay the price to obtain it.

Building Block # 5:
You cannot lead another past the place where you are.

Building Block # 6:
There are no difficult people; there are only different personalities for you to learn.

Building Block # 7:
What you think you are running away from, you are actually running toward.

Building Block # 8:
Each day you choose to either perpetuate the confusion in your life or resolve issues.

Building Block # 9:
People who work to eliminate stress become stressful; people who learn to control their stress enhance their creativity.

Building Block # 10:
Most people want honesty as long as it is not honest.

Building Block # 11:
You must respond, not react.

Building Block # 12:
All human lives collide at the point of agendas.

Building Block # 13:
A problem is a concern you didn't address yesterday.

Building Block # 14:
Passion and stamina are twins.

Building Block # 15:
Your behavior never lies.

Building Block # 16:
The #1 thing a human life wants to know is that they matter.

Building Block # 17:
A life without a dream is a life with an empty internal reservoir.

Building Block # 18:
The behavior of others in your life is consistent with your design for their lives.

Building Block # 19:
Your biggest challenge is getting beyond all your old negative emotional tapes.

Building Block # 20:
I am a spiritual person.

Laying The Foundation
For This Book

When you are moving toward an adventure you have never been through before, you are filled with desire and fear. This creates a sense of excitement and uncertainty. The results of the adventure will be designed by whether your desire or your fear lays the foundation for the journey.

During my days of working with human behavior, I had watched so many bring me their desire, talk about what they wanted to do, leave, and then, give in to their fear. It wasn't that they weren't serious about what they wanted to do; they just didn't lay the right foundation before they started the journey.

Please understand! The journey doesn't depend on others as much as it depends on your inner design. It is your inner design that will determine who you will listen to and let guide you through the unknown territory.

If you are guided by your negative fear, you will be surrounded by those who started just like you, and then gave in to their fear. The only thing they can offer is their reasons, their excuses, their negative behavior. They didn't make it to the other side, so they cannot guide you through the parts they have never been through.

If you are guided by your desire, you will seek those who have reached the other side. They walked through their doubts; they faced their worries; they handled their uncertainty and achieved their dream. These are the people who can give you insights, rather than reasons and excuses. These are the people who can help you mentally and emotionally prepare for the journey.

I understood this and as I began to prepare for my adventure into the world of professional speaking, I didn't want to be guided by the wrong people. I didn't know many, but I knew a few who were speakers. I decided I would call them and ask who they would turn to if they were me. Of the six that I called, four told me I should talk to Bill Gove.

Bill Gove? I didn't have any idea who he was. As I was checking him out, I found out he was one of the founders of the National Speaker's Association. He was known for his integrity and his honesty with audiences. To top it all off, he lived about ten minutes from me.

I remember like it was yesterday the day I called him. He answered the phone with this impeccable voice, "Bill Gove."

"Bill, this is Richard Flint. You don't know me."

Before I could finish my well-rehearsed introduction, he interrupted me and said. "Should I know you?"

Well, that through me off my prepared remarks. Without hesitation I responded, "Yes. Yes, you should know me. Bill, I want to become a professional speaker and in asking around, people tell me I should talk to you about how to achieve this."

His voice took on a tone of a teacher challenging the remarks of a student. "Why do you want to become a speaker?"

"Well," I said as I was searching for the answer. "I want to become a speaker because I think I can help people learn how to live their life with meaning."

"Live their life with meaning," came back with a tone of skepticism wrapped around the words. "What makes you think people want to change their life?"

I spent the next few minutes explaining to him my background of teaching, counseling and writing. "Bill, I just want to take the things life has taught me and offer those insights to others. I know if people will listen to me I can make a difference in their lives."

There was this long silence. "Okay, here is what I will do. Do you know where Henry's Restaurant is on Congress Avenue?"

Did I know where it was! I had breakfast there almost every morning. It was my breakfast hangout. "Yes, I know exactly where it is."

"Great, meet me there tomorrow morning at 7:00 A.M. and don't be late."

The next morning I was up and ready at five. I was so anxious and so nervous. I had outlined four pages of questions I wanted to ask him. I wanted to know everything he knew. I just knew we could get through all this at breakfast.

I arrived about 6:30 and asked Judy, the waitress I knew, if she knew Bill Gove.

"Do I know Bill Gove! Richard, everyone knows Bill Gove."

Well, everyone knew him except me. "Judy, I am suppose to meet him here this morning. When he arrives, will you point him out to me?"

"You bet!" was her response as she walked away chewing her gum with that loud smack.

It wasn't long before this gentleman entered and made his way through the drug store to the restaurant. He must have stopped and spoken to everyone in the store. My mind told me "that is Bill Gove."

4

Just about the time he arrived at the restaurant entrance, Judy came by and said. "Hey Richard, that is Bill Gove."

I stood up to introduce myself, but before I could open my mouth this hand reached out and this voice said, "You must be Richard Flint."

"Yes sir!"

"So, you want to be a professional speaker!"

With those words began a classroom I had never been in before. I didn't get to ask any of my questions. Bill spent the entire two hours quizzing me. I felt like I was being interrogated.

At the end of the two hours, he looked at me and asked, "What are you doing for breakfast next week?"

"Nothing!"

"Okay, here is my deal. I will have breakfast with you every morning next week. You take all those questions you have on those pages, get them organized and we will work through them together. Richard, if at any time I feel you are not serious about this, we won't talk anymore."

The following week was like a Ph.D. course in professional speaking. What Bill shared with me advanced my career by five years. His insights, his knowledge, his wisdom took me from being someone who was searching for direction to someone who had a plan ready to be implemented.

All during the week, I kept asking "What do I owe you for your time?"

I got the same reply all week. "We will talk about it on Friday."

My mind kept telling me, "I don't have enough money to pay this man for all he is doing for me."

On Friday we met and spent time as we had done each morning that week. As we were winding down, I looked at Bill and said, "Bill, I don't have enough money to pay you for what you have done for me. How can I repay you?"

He got the Gove look on his face, smiled, leaned in and said. "Here is how you can repay me. First, every time you have the opportunity to speak, be yourself. Richard, I watch so many who are speaking to hear themselves speak. They don't care about the audience. They are there to impress, not to help. Always be yourself. That is when you will be at your best."

He paused to make sure I was understanding what he was saying. "Second, feed your audience. I don't care if you do it with humor, with words, with research or what. Just always feed your audience. Some will be there because they had to be there, but there are those few who really want to learn. Feed those who are in front of you."

There was another pause. "Third, always be prepared. Don't cheat people by not being ready to give them your best. This is not your stage, it has been loaned to you to help others. Don't show up if you are not ready."

There was another pause and I watched as the look on his face turned to one of total compassion. "The last part of the payment is this: If you ever have a young speaker come to you, like you came to me, and you feel they are serious about the industry, give back to them like I have given to you. The greatest reward you will ever find in life is helping the mentally hungry quench their thirst."

I made a commitment to Bill to fulfill those things that would repay for his investment of time and self in me. I have never forgotten that commitment. I have taken those principles:

- *Be Yourself!*
- *Feed Your Audience*
- *Always Be Prepared*
- *Invest Yourself In Those Who Are Serious*

and made them part of my Building Blocks for my total life.

Everyone needs Building Blocks to build their life upon. If you don't have those principles in place, you will not be sure about what you are doing. Building Blocks are solid principles you believe in, act out through behavior and use to guide your decision making process. They are more than words put into a thought. They are descriptive phrases on which you can build your life.

During the years, Bill and I spent many hours talking about Building Blocks. We would sit and chat about the industry, the need for speakers who understood the meaning of the platform, and about the commitment that goes with each opportunity you are given to borrow the stage for a few minutes.

My brightest memory of Bill came my second year on the National Speaking Circuit. I was asked to speak at the National Speakers' Convention.

Jeanne Robinson came to me and said, "Richard, you are doing more business your second year than most do after ten years on the circuit. Would you share with us how you are doing it?"

I was backstage nervously pacing while waiting my turn. I looked up and there was Bill.

He smiled the "Gove" smile and asked, "Are you nervous?"

"Nervous! Bill, I am scared to death."

"What's there to be scared about? It is just another audience. So what if it is filled with your peers. So what if most of them have been speaking three times as long as you. So what if most are envious about you getting the spot on the program. It is just another audience."

He walked over, gave me a hug and offered one more piece of advice. "You are going to do great. Trust yourself. Oh, Flint, if you are ever going to screw up, don't do it now."

With that he turned, laughed out loud and disappeared. His presence calmed me down and took me back to the mission at hand. I have to tell you, I don't think I have ever been better.

When I finished, Bill was the first one to me. He smiled that "Gove" smile, hugged me and said. "Good job buddy! I knew you could do it."

That meant more to me than any applause I have ever gotten. This was my guide, giving me a mental, emotional and physical hug. How much better could life be?

All of us need those mental, emotional and physical hugs. They come in so many different forms and from many different people. Sometimes they come from those who are close to your life. They are in your life to offer you consistent support. That support is so important for the time when the pathway is not as clear as you would like it to be.

Sometimes the support comes from one who just pauses in your life for the brief time they were meant to be there. The key is to be prepared to recognize their presence and pause to learn from it.

That presence can come from one who is physically passing through your life or has entered your life through a book you have read. Many of you who read this book I will not know. Please understand *Building Blocks* is filled with mental and emotional hugs. If you can find yourself in the stories, you will understand the applications. Not all the stories will relate to where you are right now in your life. That is okay; pay attention to them, but don't dwell on them. The day will come when you will need them and that is the time for you to come back and reach deep inside for the personal connection.

Others will find immediate connection points in your life. It will be as if you have known them forever. Reflect on them; make them a focus point for your life; find their meaning and use it to improve your life.

Remember: The only time you will screw up in life is when:

- *You are not being yourself.*
- *You are not feeding those who are in your life.*
- *You are not prepared for what you've been given.*
- *You are not investing in yourself and others.*

My friend, guide and mentor died while I was writing this book. I had already decided to dedicate it to him. My sadness is I won't be able to hand him a copy, but I know he is still watching over my life. He physical body may be gone, but his spirit still lives inside of me. I can still hear that "Gove" laugh and feel his support and encouragement.

Bill Gove, thank you for investing yourself in me. I promise, as long as God gives me time, I will strive to help others understand the Building Blocks that will allow them to have a better life. Your presence is felt!

Notes

WASTED ENERGY

*Why spend your energy being a carbon copy
when you are an original!*

It was during my time as the Baptist Campus
Minister at Ohio University that I met Steve. He
was like so many college students — confused
about what he wanted to do, but working toward a
degree he really didn't want.

It was his Junior year when he asked if he
could talk to me. He arrived at my office and his
eyes said he was nervous. As he sat down, his
opening statement was "I really don't know how to
talk about this." The pause said this was a very
emotional issue and he had been wrestling with it
for some time.

"Just tell me what's going on," was my
response.

He took a deep sigh and started his journey
filled with confusion. Steve came from a very
controlling environment. His father was the
dominant figure and took control of everyone's
life. His mother was not allowed to make any
decisions; she always had to get his father's
approval. If he didn't agree, the subject was
dropped and there was no further discussion.

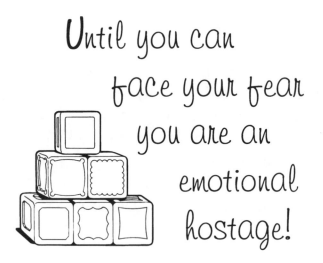

Until you can
face your fear
you are an
emotional
hostage!

Steve has two older brothers. Each had had their life planned by their father. When they went away to school, it was to fulfill the plan he had for their life. It was no different for Steve. From his childhood it was planned that Steve was to become a doctor. That was what his father saw him doing. There was no discussion with Steve whether this was what he wanted for his life. It was understood through silence that was the plan.

Steve graduated from high school and made his way to Ohio University to make his journey toward becoming a doctor. Things went fairly smoothly his freshman year. The University was a place for fun. His grades weren't what they should be, so his dad had a major talk with him. It was made clear that his time at OU was not for fun, but for study and good grades. How was he going to get into Medical School if he didn't have the grades? Steve knew better than to talk back to his father. Once, he did that, and the result was not something he wanted to go through again.

So, Steve buckled down and rose to the top of his class. Steve was a very intelligent young man, but trapped in a design that was not his. His life didn't belong to him; it was being designed and controlled by his father.

As his father put it, Steve didn't know what

was best for him. He was a foolish kid who needed someone to point him in the right direction and keep him on course.

Steve's Sophomore year saw an increase in his personal frustrations. He saw his life being taken away from him, *but* how do you tell your father this is not what you want for your life? He couldn't disappoint his father. That would be an unforgivable sin.

As he reached the halfway point of his Junior year, the stress was affecting him physically. He was always tired, couldn't sleep and saw himself moving deeper into his father's prison. A couple of times he had reached the point where he was going to talk with his father, but lost the courage when the time came. That just pushed Steve deeper into his cave of depression. Steve knew he had to do something or this was going to kill him.

Over the next three months, Steve and I worked through some very challenging questions:

- *What do you really want for your life?*
- *Why is this so important to you?*
- *Is your desire to have it strong enough to face losing your father?*

Each of these was an emotional journey.
Each time we talked, Steve reassured himself that
planning his own life was the most important thing
in his life. Each time we talked you could feel his
desire and see his fear. We both knew that, until the
desire was stronger than the fear, there was no
talking to his father.

We kept working through his dream. We
kept planning a life that belonged to him. We kept
strengthening why this was so important to him.
We kept facing the price tag and talking about
being an original. We kept visiting what would
happen if he lived his father's plan and gave up his
dream.

I will never forget the day his father came to
my office for the visit with Steve and myself. I had
agreed to be there, but not to have the conversation
for Steve. This was *his* mission. If *I* did it for him,
he would not be free from the guilt he would feel.
The freedom from the guilt could only occur when
he stepped forward and completed that of which he
was fearful. Until you can face your fear, you are
an emotional hostage!

The conversation began with Steve
stumbling through his feelings. The more he
focused on what his real desire was for his life, the
calmer he became in his ability to share with his

father.

Watching his father was an interesting thing. In the beginning you could see how upset he was with his son. Several times he tried to interrupt Steve, but Steve just kept moving forward. As the father began to see how passionate Steve was about his dream, he began to relax and listen to what his son was saying. As the conversation moved forward, Steve's father looked at him with tears in his eyes and said, "Son, I wished you had told me this sooner. All I want for you is for you to be happy. I am sorry. I didn't mean to hurt you."

Steve went forward with his dream. Today he is a science teacher and having the time of his life. The last time we talked we laughed about the pain he put himself through. His relationship with his father matured to a real friendship. The respect each had for the other made it a very special thing.

There are so many Steve's out there. The tragedy is — most never face their fear and live as a prisoner in their own life. They spend their life being what they are programmed to be, rather than being the original they were designed to become.

I see them everyday as I travel. You can look in their eyes and know they are not living. They are existing in a world that doesn't bring them happiness, doesn't offer them personal fulfillment and doesn't offer them a sense of freedom. They are trapped by their fear of facing what *is*; they are held hostage be allowing that fear to weaken their desire. They don't understand that when you live as a carbon copy, each day weakens your desire to really live your dream.

Here are some questions for you to *honestly* answer:

- *Are you doing what you really want to be doing with your life?*

- *What would you do differently with your life if you weren't afraid?*

- *What would it take for you to face your fear, move beyond it and you become an original?*

The Process To Becoming An Original:

O *open yourself to what is really happening in your life*

R *refuse to continue to run from your fear*

I *invest your energy in your dream; it is there*

G *get clear on the price involved in moving forward*

I *invest your time and energy in feeding your desire*

N *no longer listen to the negative soothsayers*

A *allow yourself to take the risk*

L *let your imagination guide you; not negative emotions*

What if you got to the end of your life and the only thing that could be said about you was, he/she lived their life and didn't feel fulfilled by the life they lived? Why spend your energy being a carbon copy when you were created to be an original? It is your choice to face or deny!

You Are Responsible

You are perfectly designed to achieve what you are achieving.

Patty approached me as I finished my program in St. Cloud, Minnesota. I had noticed her in the audience, because she seemed very uncomfortable with what I was talking about.

My topic had been *Do You Really Want It?* This program examines the inconsistencies in a human life and focuses on the world of excuses. It really hits hard at why people make excuses and give reasons for why there is so much confusion in their lives.

As she approached, her opening words were "You are a very difficult person to like."

I said, "Really! Why do you say that?"

"You have the ability to see right through a person. I saw you watching me today. You knew I was the person you were describing. My life is so far out of sync I don't think I can ever get back."

I had a few minutes, so I asked her to sit down and tell me about her life. That was all she needed to open her emotional vault, which had become a dumping ground, rather than a recycling center. Any time you don't face what is happening in your life you *store* all your emotional garbage,

*B*lame gives you permission to stay the same, and grants you permisson to play the pity game.

rather than let it go. Over a period of time it creates the frustrations and confusion you drag throughout your day. This creates a consistent drain on your life and just keeps wearing you down.

Her story was not a new one. She had grown up in a home where there was very little love and affection. Since she was the oldest of four, she was expected to take care of her brother and sisters. Her dad was a long haul truck driver who was gone for weeks at a time. When he was home, all he did was drink and sleep. Her mother did the best she could do, working as a waitress from early evening to midnight.

Patty was never allowed to be a child. She was forced to be an adult in a child's body. Having missed childhood, Patty missed most of the self discovery time.

I wish parents understood the concept of letting a child be a child. Research tells us when a child misses childhood, they miss the most important years of their development. When they miss childhood, they don't develop their ability to laugh or cry. When they miss childhood, their social skills are not what they should be.

Patty was a great example of that. She was an old person in a young person's body. She wrestled with who she was, what her life was about and how to have a meaningful relationship with another person.

As she talked, you could feel her emotional pain. As she told her story, you could sense her anger. As she talked through her life, you could see the confusion that surrounded her life.

The majority of her sharing was her blaming the others who had passed through her life for all the problems she had. She blamed her father; she blamed her mother; she blamed her ex-husband; she blamed her boss who knew her financial struggles and used it to hold her hostage. They were the reason her life was so messed up.

She got really upset with me when I began to ask her some personally revealing questions:

• *Do you still live at home?*

Her reply was "no."

"Then Patty, why do you continue to blame your father or mother?"

"Because of what they did to me!"

"Patty, that was yesterday, not today. You get to decide who you are today. You don't have to continue to replay that old tape. You have a choice here."

• *Are you still married to your ex-husband?*

Her reply was "no."

"Then Patty, why do you still blame him for the lack of a relationship in your life?"

"Because of the emotional scars he left me with. He made me hate men."

"But Patty, he is only one man. You are making him every man. That is just another justification for not facing the real issues that are here."

• *Does your boss force you to work here?*

Her reply was "no."

"Then Patty, why is he the issue?

"Because he knows I need a job. If I quit, I won't have a job and I am not sure I can find another one."

"Are you talented?"

"I don't know. There are times I know I am and there are other times I am not sure."

"Staying or leaving is your choice."

There was a long moment of silence and then she said. "What you're saying is I am the problem."

"No! What I am saying is you are the *solution*. Patty, you are perfectly designed to achieve what you are achieving. Your life is the result of your design. Each decision you make creates the journey you will make. No one forces you to live the life you are living. This life is your

25

choice created by your design. Blaming others is simply your way of avoiding facing the decisions you have made. As long as you blame others, you stay trapped in your emotional prison. Freedom from this emotional prison demands you realize that it is your design acted out through your behavior."

Patty's life is the rule, rather than the exception. Most want to make others responsible for who they aren't and what they haven't achieved with their life. Reality is — it is your life; you have designed what it is; you are the responsible party.

Blame is avoidance; blame is another way of justifying what you don't want to face; blame gives you permission to stay the same, and grants you permission to play the pity game. As long as you make "them" your reason, you don't have to be accountably responsible for your behavior.

You are perfectly designed to achieve what you are achieving. You have to understand that. It is your life; who you are is the result of the decisions you have made or have allowed others to make for you. When you give away control of your life, don't blame them for what is. They are simply doing what you have given them permission to do.

You are perfectly designed to achieve what you are achieving. Look at yourself. Every decision you make creates a journey. That journey takes you in a direction. That direction either brings clarity or confusion to your life. If you don't like the results of the journey, you have the right to redesign it. It is not the responsibility of others to redesign your life. If they do and you follow their design, you are an actor in their play. That means you have given up control of your life. Don't blame them! They are in control of your life because you have granted them that place.

Here are some questions for you to *honestly* answer:

- *Do you blame others for the struggles you have in your life?*

- *Have you given others the right to make decisions for you?*

- *Have you taken responsibility for the design of your life?*

How Do You Redesign Your Life When You Realize What You Have Done?

R *refuse to continue to live blaming others*

E *emotionally slow down*

D *decide what it is you are blaming others for*

E *examine why the blame is there*

S *search for a lesson the event has given you*

I *invest the lesson in a revised story*

G *get beyond the pain of yesterday*

N *never make others accountable for your behavior*

YOU AS A CONTRADICTION

If what you say you want is contradicted by what you do, then you are lying to yourself and all you have said it to.

He was one of those people I got to experience, but never got to meet. He appeared, spoke and was gone. To this day I don't know his name.

I was in St. Louis at the Adams Mark Hotel to speak for Amway/Quixtar. I was excited to be there. It was an evening filled with people whose energy was just pounding. The challenge was the design of the evening schedule. I was scheduled to speak at 8:00 P.M. for 90 minutes. It didn't take long for them to get behind schedule. There were some speakers who either couldn't tell time or just didn't care they were stealing from those who were behind them.

Anyway, by the time they got around to me it was 11:25 P.M. Now, I know you would have still been awake and in your seat waiting for my presentation. Realizing the lateness of the hour and feeling for the people who had been there since 6:00 P.M., I decided to take twenty one minutes and share with them information I consider to be the #1

A life that is driven by contradictions becomes a life that is trapped in the Circle of Sameness.

issue you must face if you want to grow —
personal honesty.

I learned, when I was doing private
counseling, that most people don't face their life
with honesty. It is too risky for them. They know if
they do, they are going to have to become
accountable for what is happening in their life. It is
so much easier for them to just lie to self and
others. They feel it saves them a lot of pain.
Reality is — it causes them much more anguish
and personal frustration.

The next morning I was at breakfast. If you
know me, you know I don't sleep very much. My
rest requirements are four hours. That means I am
a very early riser. Normally, I am the first one in
the restaurant. I was enjoying my coffee and
working on an article when I spotted him.

He was standing in the corner watching me.
After 20 years of watching and studying people,
you can figure out what they are going to do. I
knew he needed to talk, and I had been chosen to
be the recipient of his words. I figured by the time
I got my computer shut down he would be at my
table.

Just as I closed the lid to my computer, he
was at my table. He stood there for a minute just
staring at me. I figured he either didn't know

where to start or was wondering if he should really do this.

He closed his eyes, took a deep breath and said, "Can I talk to you?"

I smiled and replied, "Sure." I pointed to a chair and continued, "sit down."

He stepped back got this stern look on his face, "No! I didn't say I wanted to sit with you. I just need to talk to you."

I guess he read the surprise on my face. The stern look melted a little, but he continued. "I was in your audience last night and your little talk is the reason I couldn't sleep. I sat up all night arguing with you."

His look turned to one of near anger. "How could you talk to me like that? Yes, I have told people I want to be successful with this. No, it wasn't the truth, but I wasn't going to tell them that. I could do this if I chose to, but I just wanted to see what it was all about."

He paused and the anger turned to a deep look of pain. "That has been my way of living for years. I am good at starting things, but never completing them. I get excited and then seem to lose interest. I brag to others about what I am going to accomplish and then have to stay away because I don't ever do it. My wife says I spend all my time lying to myself. She just laughs when I come up with something new I am going to do."

He paused again, looked at me with disgust and continued. "Reality is, I have been lying to myself for forty years and you or no one else is going to change that fact!"

With that he turned and walked out of my life. As he walked away my mind was racing with what had just happened. I took out my legal pad and wrote this thought. *If what you say you want is contradicted by what you do, then you are lying to yourself and all you have said it to.*

Would you agree that is the truth?

How much confusion is created by living in a world of good intentions? You find something that piques your interest, jump into it and then exit before you have finished the journey.

How much frustration do you think you create for others when you tell them what you are going to do, they take what you are saying as fact and then, you don't deliver? After a period of time do you think they stop believing what you say?

Most don't realize just because you quit doesn't mean your mind stops working on what it has started. Your mind doesn't file anything until it has been completed. Each thing you start, but don't complete, remains an open file your mind thinks about, keeps pulling out and reminding you of.

The result of a life that doesn't complete is a life that is scattered. Everywhere you look there are mental, emotional and physical stacks that steal energy.

The result of a life that doesn't complete is a life that frustrates others who are depending on them. People want to believe what you tell them, *but* if your behavior says you can't be trusted to do what you have promised to do, they soon just stop believing in you.

The result of a life that doesn't complete what it starts is a life that is always tired from wrestling with time. Those who don't finish are always having to justify to themselves or others why things are not getting done. It is time consuming and very draining.

A life that is driven by contradictions becomes a life that is trapped in the Circle of Sameness. It can't move forward; it can only move in circles. Even if it starts something new, it cannot move forward. There are too many unfinished items hanging around as mental residue. The mental residue makes it impossible for the mind to stay focused on what is in front of it. The stacks keep calling out for attention. If the stacks involve others, then there are all the fires to fight. Each day is a series of moments where you touch things to keep them from becoming a bond fire, rather than completing things so you can move forward.

A life that is driven by contradictions is a life that soon loses the trust others had for them. It is impossible to trust someone who keeps creating contradictions. Why would you expect someone to believe in you when your behavior keeps creating their disappointments? When people can no longer trust in you, they no longer want to be around you.

Most who are like this gentleman are controlled by the fear of failure or the fear of rejection. Their behavior is that of a person who doesn't have a solid foundation to build on. They start out filled with excitement, but become trapped when the excitement is replaced by fear they don't know how to confront. Negative fear kills excitement. Negative fear creates such a feeling of uncertainty that you are trapped in a world of "what if."

That world creates a person who talks big, but lives small. Their life becomes a series of statements that are constantly contradicted by their behavior.

Contradictions are mentally paralyzing. They take mental energy that could be given to events that will push your life forward, rather than stealing energy that leaves you exhausted.

Here are some questions for you to *honestly* answer:

- *Do you start things you don't intend to complete?*

- *Do you live in a world where stacks steal your energy?*

- *When you tell someone you are going to do something, do they see you as a person they can trust?*

- *Is yours a life of contradictions?*

How Do You Stop Lying To Yourself?

S *stay focused on the "now"*

T *take inventory of the stacks that now exist*

O *organize yourself to take action*

P *pause periodically and study your behavior*

WATCH WHAT YOU SAY
Don't tell me what you want if you are not willing to pay the price to obtain it.

Life is not controlled by your wishes or your desires; it is controlled by the price you are willing to pay to achieve your dream. It is at the point of price tag where most lives unravel.

Little did I know when I met him that John was going to be one of the most challenging people I ever agreed to work with. I met him in Colorado Springs while I was speaking for a group of Automotive Repair Owners.

My topic was *Understanding The Psychology of Improvement.* Most people don't improve, because they are too busy wrestling with change. My mission was to walk these business owners through the Improvement Process. I had invited one of the business owners I had worked with to share his journey with them. He spent his time showing them the transition he had to make to remove the concept of change and replace it with the process of improvement.

What I have found is that most people want to improve as long as they can call the shots. They don't understand the process that removes the

Most people don't improve, because they are too busy wrestling with change.

concept of change and replaces it with the process of improvement. They look at any new idea as a change they are going to have to make. When change takes center stage, most are going to find a reason to resist it. Too many believe in the idea of working to become comfortable. What they fail to realize is — becoming comfortable can stand in the way of continuing to improve.

The major piece of information is showing them how information enters a life. It has two entrance points: your emotions and your mind. If information enters your life through your emotional filtering system, it has to work its way through all your old tapes. With each event you have had in your life you make a tape which defines the event's meaning to your life. Most of those tapes are filled with negative perceptions. That means the most positive event can unravel as it passes through your negative filters. When it gets through to the other side, you find yourself wrestling with what these changes are going to do to your life.

The other informational entrance point is through your mind. Information that enters through this portal passes through your imagination. Since your imagination is the most positive point in your life, all information that enters here is processed through the world of possibility. This creates a sense of excitement and energy for your life.

Your mind is such an interesting machine. It is impossible for it to have a negative day. It works in a world of resolution. With each event your mind views, it sees the other side and what great things can happen to your life.

The great battle for control of your life is created by who you are listening to. If you listen through your emotions, you are constantly trying to understand the meaning of change. If you listen through your mind, you are seeing the rewards that come with being a risk taker.

John was interesting because he was a contradiction. What he saw on the outside was not what lived on the inside. He had been to enough programs that he knew the right words. He had the lingo down pat.

When he approached me, his opening words were "I need you to fix my life."

I smiled and replied, "Whoops! You have come to the wrong person. I gave up fixing lives years ago."

He smiled, chuckled and continued. "No, I am serious. I know what I want, but I don't know how to get there. I've talked to some of the people you have worked with and you're the guy to fix my life."

"John," I said. "I cannot fix anyone's life. I can guide people to implementing the processes that will improve their life, *but* I cannot fix anyone's life."

"Okay," he said with this look of impatience on his face. "How long will it take you to improve my life."

"Whoops," I said. "Wrong choice of words. I cannot improve your life. I can guide you to the steps necessary for you to improve your life, *but* I cannot improve your life for you."

You could tell I was not saying what he wanted to hear. "I know what I want, but I don't know how to get there. Can you help me improve my life and get to where I want to be?"

"Hey," I said. "I think you are getting it. If you really want it and are willing to stretch yourself through taking the risk that will push you out of your comfort zone, I can help you."

That started a journey that was supposed to last a year that ended after three months. For three months I would challenge the design he was using for his life to be greeted with "Why do I have to do that. Things are just fine the way they are."

"Because," I would say, "this is one of the improvements you need to make to make it to the other side."

"Yea, but that means a lot of work. Why can't we just skip this part and move on to something that doesn't require as much emotional work?"

After three months of hearing every reason why he didn't think he needed to do the things that had to be done, I ended the relationship.

I remember standing in his office informing him I had chosen to end my coaching relationship with him. The look on his face was one of disbelief.

"Listen," he said. "I really want this, but what you are asking is just too tough. I thought this was going to be a simple thing of tweaking this and straightening that. I didn't know it was going to be this much effort."

"John," I replied, "Here is the real issue we are facing. You want the end result without paying the price. It doesn't work that way. There is a price tag to everything you want to achieve with your life. You can only go as far as the price tag is acceptable. When the price tag is too great, you quit. There is no doubt you think you really want to improve your life, but you will never have it until you are willing to pay the price. Don't stand here and tell me what you want if you are not willing to pay the price to have it."

I saw him not long ago and ask him "How are you doing?" He looked at me with pain in his eyes and said, "About the same. I have gotten so close and had things fall apart. It is like I am my own worst enemy."

"You are," I said. "It goes back to the conversation we had about the price tag. You cannot improve your life until you understand and agree to the price tag that goes with the journey. John, it's that price tag that controls the journey, not what you think you want."

Does this make sense to you? You can have the greatest idea in the world, but if you aren't willing to pay the price to obtain it, it goes away.

This price tag is about discipline. If you are scattered, or one who can't finish what you start, the price tag is always going to be a point of conflict with you.

This price tag is about commitment. If you are a free spirit who is driven by the excitement of the moment and not the commitment to the journey, you are always going to sit down when the price tag goes beyond your willingness to step forward.

This price tag is about risk taking. If you are a person who has to live in a predictable world, you will always balk when you are asked to step out of your comfort zone.

In life you will always find things that excite you. That excitement will cause you to want to explore whether this could be the right place for you. That excitement you are feeling will be controlled by how far you are willing to stretch. That willingness to stretch is the price tag. When you reach the limit you are willing to stretch, the price tag is too great. At that point the journey ends and the excuses and reasons take over.

Here are some questions for you to *honestly* answer:

- *Are you a risk taker?*

- *Do you start things before you consider the mental and emotional price tags involved?*

- *Do you get excited, start things and then lose interest?*

Paying The Price Demands:

P *patience*

R *realistic dream*

I *information gathering*

C *commitment & discipline*

E *educating yourself on what is involved*

Notes

Leadership With Others
You cannot lead another past the place
where you are.

All people have value! I listen to people put
themselves down and know they don't see
themselves as a person who brings value. All
people have something to offer, but not all people
see it.

When a person accepts the role of leader,
they make a promise to those they are there to
lead. That promise is about presence. It says, "I
can help you improve and commit my knowledge
and expertise to you." That is a very serious
promise and has given rise to one of the biggest
lies in the world of leadership.

My years of working with leadership has
shown me that most are not leaders; they are there
to manage the fires they face each day. Being a fire
fighter negates leadership. Why?

You take on the problems others have
created and handed over to the leader to take care
of. When the leader becomes a participant in the
fire, they leave the role of leader. The fire should
be given back to those who created it. As long as
they are protected from facing the messes they
create, they will continue to repeat the behavior

When a leader stops learning, their value diminishes.

that creates the fires.

Leadership is also negated because fighting fires drains you emotionally. You cannot spend your days fighting the fires without it costing you energy. A problem is a concern that was not addressed when things were calm and being questioned. Most problems are not handed to the leader until they become a crisis. In a crisis emotions are running high and people are reacting and not communicating. Without clear communication nothing gets resolved!

Leadership is negated because fighting fires steals your time. Do you ever come in early or stay late to finish your day? Do you ever plan agendas for the day you don't get to because of the surprises you are handed?

When the fire captures your day, other things have to be put aside. It doesn't mean they don't need to be done; it simply says you can't get to them as you had planned. Does that create an emotional reaction?

The role of any leader is to provide leadership. That sounds so simple, but it becomes the greatest challenge most leaders face. When there is no leadership, the company (which is the environment people are in) is adrift.

The role of leadership is to hold people

accountable for their behavior. When one is not made accountable for what they do, it validates and gives them permission to continue what they have done. That weakens the presence of leadership and costs them the respect of those who are looking to them for growth.

I was in San Francisco speaking on *No Excuse Management* when I met Steve and Judy. They owned a medium-sized sales company in the Midwest. They asked if I had any time to talk to them, so we agreed to meet for breakfast the next morning.

When we got together, Judy did most of the talking. It was interesting listening to her talk and watching Steve sit there. The issue was the lack of leadership in the company. They didn't have a challenge attracting salespeople; their challenge was keeping them. When I questioned the challenge with keeping the people, the response was, "They soon realize we lied to them."

That made me sit up and pay attention. I asked for clarification and Judy responded. "When we talk to them we talk to them about our commitment to training. We assure them we will train them. Then, when they get on board, we don't follow through."

She paused, looked at Steve and continued.

"It is Steve's role to train them. He does great with the new salespeople who don't know anything, but when we get an experienced salesperson, he doesn't work with them."

I turned to Steve and asked, "Is Judy's assessment of this correct?"

He looked at her and then stared back at me. "Yes, she is right. I enjoy working with the new people. They are hungry and want to learn. They have very little, if any, knowledge and listen to all I say."

There was a long pause before he continued. "The experienced salespeople are a different story. They have a different level of need. My problem is my lack of up-to-date selling. I have been out of the field for several years now and my knowledge is not what it used to be. I don't feel comfortable trying to train them. Most of them know more than I do."

Right there we discovered the real issue. When one is in leadership and knows they lack the leadership ability, they tend to shy away from the experienced players. They feel they don't bring much value to the table. So, rather than stepping up and becoming a student, they back away and lose presence and respect.

The time design of most in leadership does

not include time as a student. Yet, any great leader understands you cannot lead another past the point where you are. That thought demands that every leader continue their journey as a student. When a leader stops learning, their value diminishes.

This is not saying you must always know more than your people, *but* that you be able to bring value to the table. The value of your presence is one of the things that makes people want to sit in your presence. When people feel you have something to offer, they will pause and ask you to be their teacher. When they feel you have nothing to offer, they will bypass your presence and seek one who can be their teacher.

This fact has cost so many organizations their quality people. Those seeking growth are looking for a teacher. Those who are wanting to improve are seeking guidance. Those who are wanting to find the next dimension are looking for a mentor. The leader should have a presence that says *I am here to strengthen, guide and help you improve.*

This has been lost in companies that see the leader as the protector of the bottom line, rather than the developer of the people. I am not sure how it happened, but we have lost sight of the bottom line being a result, rather than a creation.

Managing the bottom line has made many in the leadership position lazy learners. They don't see the need to continue their own growth journey. Therefore, they lose presence with their growth-oriented people and become the protector of those who are the company arsonist. The result is a company with the wrong focus and the wrong people.

Here are some questions for you to *honestly* answer:

- *Are you a leader or a fire fighter?*

- *Is there time for your growth in your daily schedule?*

- *Do you lack the skills necessary to take your people forward?*

For The Leader To Be The Teacher They Must:

L *listen to their people's experiences*
E *examine their learning needs*
A *always remain a student*
D *develop themselves*

Notes

No Difficult People

*There are no difficult people; there are only
different personalities for you to learn.*

Of all the research and program writing I
have done over twenty plus years *A Day At The
Zoo* still remains my favorite program to deliver. I
spent five years researching and writing it. I have
great respect for what animals can teach us.

For years I had listened to people use the
statement *working here is like working in a zoo. I
just don't understand why I attract all the crazy
animals.* One day my mind said "let's see if we can
do something with this."

That started a five year journey of visiting
zoos, talking to those who worked with the
animals and learning the uniqueness of the
animals' personalities. Each time I learned about
an animal, I would see the faces of people I knew.
It became the most insightful learning experience I
had ever been through. Each time I have the
opportunity to share the research with an audience,
their eyes light up, their minds come alive and they
leave with a picture of human behavior they will
never forget.

When you lack time and patience, all people are going to appear difficult!

The thought that guides the program states *there are no difficult people; there are only different personalities for you to invest your time and energy in understanding.* That statement makes people stop and think. How many times have you classified someone as difficult? How many times have you avoided someone because you didn't want to face their behavior? How many times have you written someone off because of your perception about them?

I was speaking to the Club Managers National Convention in Las Vegas when Peter arrived in my life. I had finished the Zoo Program and was packing up. Everyone had left the room except for Peter. I could see by the look on his face he was struggling with something.

I stopped, looked at him and said, "You look like you have a question. Ask me."

He walked over, sat down, looked at me for a second and said, "I have a real problem with a statement you made. You said 'there are no difficult people.' I don't think I agree with that."

"Why?" was my response.

"Because there have been people in my life I just couldn't get along with. I don't care how much I tried to help them, they were just difficult."

That started a two hour conversation helping

him to understand the psychological difference between "difficult" and "different." Most people find it easier to make someone difficult, rather than see them as a different personality.

For many, classifying someone as "difficult" gives them permission to avoid that person or have a reason to write them off. It creates the excuse they are searching for to avoid facing the real issue that is there.

The term "difficult" really becomes a catch word. It is used whenever one doesn't want to confront, invest time in or work with a person. I have seen it used over and over again as a justification for avoidance behavior.

"Hey," I said. "Let me ask you some questions."

"Okay!"

"What is a day of your life like? Are there more things to get done than you have time to do?"

"Yes! That describes most days of my life. I start with good intentions, but the minute I walk in, I am handed a situation that usually takes my day away from me."

"Are you a really patient person?"

He smiled and let out a half laugh. "How can you be patient when you are running the entire day? I think I remember one time when I was patient, but it was so long ago it is like a blur."

"Do you have a staff you can depend on?"

His pause told me he was running each of his staff people through his mind. "Not really. I have five and there is only one I can depend on. The rest you have to prod, push or pull. They are not self-motivated and wait for me to tell them what to do. Most of the time I have to tell them the same thing two or three times."

"Let me ask you one more question. Do you manage your environment or does it manage you?"

"Oh," he said without any hesitation. "It definitely manages me. You know they call me a department head, but I am not. I am the department tail. I spend most of my time chasing myself. I get so exhausted trying to find people and checking on whether they are getting things done."

There was this long pause and he continued. "That is why I don't think I can agree with your statement. Those people are not there to work; they are not there to make my life easier; they are there to keep me upset. They are really a group of difficult people."

I moved closer to him so I could look him squarely in the eye. "You have to hear the entire thought, not just part of it. These people appear difficult to you because you are lacking the two

major aspects of working effectively with people
— time and patience."

I paused to let him grasp what I was saying.
"You have said you don't have time. Time and
patience go hand in hand. If you don't have time,
you are not going to be a very patient person. You
have said you don't manage the environment; it
manages you. That makes you a person who is out
of control. That means you spend more time
reacting to what is not happening than you do
responding to what is happening."

I paused to make sure he was still with me.
"Do you understand what I am saying? It is not the
fact that these people are difficult. The reality is,
you don't have the time to be patient enough to
deal with what is happening. Therefore, the easy
answer is that your people are difficult."

He looked at me with this look that said he
was getting what I was saying. "I understand what
you are saying. I don't walk with my people. I ask
and expect my people to run with me. Not all of
them are willing to do that. That frustrates me and
makes me very upset with them. Maybe I need to
learn how to slow down and, rather than live in a
crisis driven world, start living in a world where I
learn to walk with people."

I smiled at him and said, "I think you are

beginning to get the picture. 'Difficult' is our catch word for people for whom we don't have time and patience to slow down and understand."

There really are no difficult people. There are only different people for you to slow down and invest your time and your energy in understanding. If you don't understand them, you will not know how to connect with them. If you cannot connect with them, you will push them to the corner of your life and get frustrated each and every time you look at them. The only way you will learn how to use their presence in your life is to slow down, give them your time and energy and create a common agenda that allows you to move with them.

Granted, there will be some people who enter your life who will refuse to let you understand them. They are people who stand outside your life, not in your life. They are people who don't want to be part of anything you do; they only want to stand outside and offer comments and criticism. They are not difficult; they are defiant. You should not stand in their presence. The best thing is to face the fact of who they are, eliminate them and move forward. If you pause with these people, they will suck the life out of you. They are dangerous; they are very intelligent; they are masters at bringing out the emotional worst in you. Eliminate them! Spend your time with those you can lead through the investment of your time and patience.

Here are some questions for you to *honestly* answer:

- *Are you a patient person?*

- *Do you live at a pace you can manage?*

- *Do you ever classify people as "difficult" in order to avoid them?*

How Do You Learn To Find The Best In A Person?

P *pace is critical*

E *emotionally stay calm*

R *refuse to react to their behavior*

S *stay with them, not ahead of them*

O *open yourself to learning about them*

N *notice what they do right*

RUNNING AWAY

*What you think you are running away from, you
are actually running toward.*

I met James and Joyce at their National
Convention in Scottsdale. James approached me
after my presentation and we talked about my
speaking for his group in Ohio.

While I was in Ohio, we talked about my
Private Coaching program. It was apparent their
lives were trapped in the Circle of Sameness, and
they needed to break out. I could see the pain in
both of their eyes and the relief when I agreed to
work with them for a year.

Let me tell you about them. Joyce's
background was filled with people who used her
emotionally and abused her physically. She was
one of the most frightened people I had ever met.
She had learned how to hide within herself. She
had this huge gate around her life and wasn't going
to let anyone in. When someone started getting too
close, she would lock the gate and withdraw into
her own self-constructed prison. Then, she would
get lonely, reach out to someone, get frightened
and race back into the prison. This was her pattern
for having relationships. As we examined her life,

Every human has a
hiding place they
run to when
they are
fearful.

we couldn't find one healthy relationship she had ever had. Every relationship became an emotional nightmare stacked on top of the previous one.

James had grown up in an environment where nothing he ever did was good enough. He is very intelligent, very talented and highly insecure. From his childhood he developed the behavior of always feeling he had to prove how good he was. This created a lifestyle of one collision after another. Everything he tried ended up being a disaster. Then, he would not stay around to face what had happened. He would pack his life and run away. The next place he arrived it didn't take long for the process to be repeated. This was the pattern for his life.

Now, put the two of them together in a relationship. Here is Joyce with her wall and locked gate, living with James who doesn't feel he is good at anything, including his relationship with Joyce, trying to prove to her he loves her. What kind of picture does that paint in your mind of their relationship?

When we began to talk about this in our sessions, neither were willing to admit they were that way. It took five months of consistent personal examples for them to open themselves to the possibility they were avoiding facing their lives.

I remember one specific conversation we had that was so revealing. I asked James, "What happens when you try to get close to Joyce?"

"Let's see," he said as he stared at her. "She enjoys it for a little while and then seems to run away."

"James, how does that make you feel?"

"I feel I am being punished for something I didn't do."

"What else?"

"I feel I am not good enough for her life. I just want to run away."

"Do you run away?"

"Yes, I go to my cave."

In the beginning of our time together I talked to them about the concept of running away. I tried to explain to them this thought: *what you think you are running from, you are actually running toward.* At first it didn't make sense to them, but over the months they began to understand what I was talking about.

We spent hours talking about where each of them ran to. Joyce ran to her prison. That was where she felt safe; in the prison no one could get to her. It took many discussions for her to realize that in the prison she shared emotional space with all the people she was running away from.

James ran to his cave. When he was small, there was this cave near his house he would go to when things were bad at home. He would go there and sit in the dark, because he knew no one could see him. There he didn't have to prove anything. In the cave people didn't reject him.

"Joyce, what happens when James starts getting too close?"

"I get scared and run into my prison. I am so afraid he is going to treat me like the others have treated me. They pretend to love me and then they hurt me. I am so tired of being hurt."

"Let me ask both of you a question. What happens when you run away? Does anything get resolved?"

They looked at each other, looked at me and responded. "NO!"

"Richard, I am so tired of that cave. I don't want to go there anymore, but it has become my behavior. I have been there so long, I don't know if I can stop myself from going there."

"I feel the same way about my prison. I don't want to hide there, but it just happens. When the fears happen, it is an automatic response. I open my eyes and I am there. I know it hurts him. I know he takes it personally, *but* it has nothing to do with him. It is my past controlling my today. I am so exhausted from doing this. I just wish I could stop running and settle into a life that wasn't tiring."

That became our mission. Our journey became one of understanding what they were running from. The fear they were both wrestling with was not what caused them to run; it simply became the trigger to run to the cave or the prison. Each time they ran they weren't running away from what was happening; they were running back toward what had already happened. Each time they arrived in the cave or the prison they strengthened the power of those old negative tapes in their life. That meant the next time the fear triggered the response, it became easier to run. Over a period of years it had just become standard behavior. They didn't challenge it; they simply gave in to it.

Very few people understand the power of the old negative tapes that live within each of us. Those tapes create most of your perceptions about life. You really don't see what *is*; you see what you *perceive* to be happening. That perception is the result of the filtering system you use. If each event is filtered through yesterday's negative tapes — which are defined by pain, hurt, fear or any of a number of negative emotions — they create the perception of more of the same. Rather than slowing down and facing what is happening, you revert to old behavior which is to run away.

You know this. Every time you run, you are not running away from anything. If you were, you wouldn't continue to face those issues over and over in your life. Each time you run, you are actually running toward where you have already been. There is nothing new in running back to where you have already been. That is filled with all the things you think you are running away from. Each time you return, you just strengthen the emotions that have dragged you back there.

You must understand why running becomes so easy. Each time the old negative tapes take over, you give up control of your life. Those old negative tapes are controlled by all the bad things you think have happened in your life. When they start flashing on your memory screen, you emotionally speed up. When you emotionally speed up, you stop living in the now and start reliving yesterday. That yesterday is filled with a false sense of security. You tell yourself you are safe there, when in reality, returning there just traps you more.

The key is, every time you feel you are speeding up *you must slow down.* The issue is not

the event you are facing; it is the emotional speed
at which you are moving. The faster you move
emotionally, the less understanding you have about
what is happening.

When you slow down, you give your mind
time to participate. When your mind gets involved
it brings reason and understanding. Your mind can
show you the pathway to resolution. It can show
you how to handle the event and not avoid it.

Your emotions feed your confusion.
Anytime you feel fearful or uncertain you will
search for a place where you feel secure. 99.9% of
the time, that is yesterday. You must realize that
yesterday is an illusion. You are never safe in
yesterday. It is not reality; it is a perception you
create to avoid facing what is actually happening
in your life. As long as you use it as your room of
escape and hiding, you must repeat what it is you
think you are running from. Freedom comes when
you can slow down and face what is really
happening. Only at that point can you redesign
your behavior and start the journey toward
personal freedom.

Here are some questions for you to *honestly* answer:

- *Is there anything in your life you are running from?*

- *Do you have a hiding place where you go to avoid facing issues?*

- *Does it get tiring facing the same situations over and over?*

How Do You Learn To Stop Running Away?

L   listen to what your mind is trying to tell you

E   examine the real issue that creates the need to run

A   align yourself with someone who can help you understand

R   refuse to speed up

N   negate the old tapes through learning what you fear

Notes

YOUR DAILY CHOICE

*Each day you choose to either perpetuate the
confusion in your life or resolve issues.*

As much as some don't want to admit it, life
really is the result of the choices you make. Each
choice carries with it a journey. You face the issue,
make a choice and get the journey that goes with
the decision. If you don't like the journey,
remember that you made the choice. It is your
design.

Choices are interesting. Some are pure
guesses. You aren't sure what to do, so you take a
deep breath and go for it. Others are the result of
the research you have done. You look at the
situation, research what your options are and make
a decision.

Every situation carries with it right and
wrong questions. If you ask the wrong questions,
you get confusion and a dead end street. The dead
end street is arriving at the end of the road and
having no place to turn. For most, that means
repeating the same situation over again in their
life. The result is disappointment and being
emotionally drained.

If you ask the right question, you resolve the
issue and get to move forward in your life. Moving

Avoiding anything does not give you breathing space. It actually emotionally chokes you.

forward offers you a sense of purpose and freedom. It releases you from the Circle of Sameness. It adds calmness and clarity to your life.

The calmer you are, the easier it is for you to continue to ask the right questions and keep the journey moving in a growth direction. The more clarity you have, the easier it is to sift through all the options and opinions that you are handed.

In working with human behavior I have found it interesting how many know they have made the wrong decision, but refuse to admit it. They would rather continue to move in what they know is the wrong direction, than face the fact they "goofed," turn around and move back to center.

All decisions create a journey. The journey either feeds the confusion in your life or resolves the issue you are facing.

One of my favorite get away places in the world is the island of St. Thomas. I love to go there and hide from the world. My favorite place to stay is the Frenchman's Reef. It is a hotel that sits on the point that enters the harbor. It gives you a great view of the town and the water. I have spent many mornings watching the sun come up and just enjoying the gift of another day.

Several years ago I was there for some r & r. It had been one of those quarters where every day found me in another city. As much fun as that is, it can also become exhausting.

The third morning I was there I had gotten up very early to do some writing and watch the sun say its "Good Morning." Around seven I made my way to the restaurant for breakfast. I was shown to my table, took my seat, said good morning to the people around me and began to enjoy my coffee.

There was a couple to my right and a couple to my left. I had noticed the lady to my left didn't seem very comfortable. Within minutes after my coffee arrived, she started coughing. As I looked at her, she was more red than any person I had ever seen. There in the middle of the restaurant she threw her chair back and started jumping up and down.

I was startled by what was happening. The entire time her husband was dying with laughter. Well, the gentleman at the table to my right didn't think it was funny. He threw his chair back, raced over to where she was, stood behind her, reached his arms around her and started to squeeze her.

When she felt his arms go around her, she let out the loudest scream you have ever heard. It startled him and he dropped her.

I don't know which one of them was the reddest. He said, "Please forgive me. I thought you were choking."

She looked up at him from the floor where she was now sitting and said. "No! I've got a roach up my pant leg and I can't get it out."

Just about that time the biggest roach I have ever seen came racing out of her pant leg and scurried across the floor.

Her husband was now almost on the floor from laughter. She looked at him with a look of total disgust and said. "Well, just don't sit there. Kill it!"

He got up out of his chair, walked over to the roach that was trying to escape and planted his foot in the middle of it.

Needless the say, the entire restaurant was now tuned in to what was happening. It was about the time of the roach's demise that the Maitre'd arrived. He looked at the gentleman who was still standing over the lady, the lady who was still sitting in the floor and the husband who was standing next to the roach that didn't get away.

Looking at the lady, he said. "Is there a problem?"

She looked up at him, pointed toward the remains of the roach and said in a not too friendly voice, "I had a roach up my pant leg."

The Maitre'd made his way over to the

roach, leaned over and gave it a good look, turned back to the lady and said. "Just a little one; just a little one."

I am here to tell you that roach was as big as any roach I had ever seen. I didn't know who to feel the worse for:

- the lady who had the challenge with the roach,
- or the man who thought she was choking.

Here was a situation where there was confusion created by the man not knowing all the facts. He saw a situation, surmised what was happening, made a decision and took action—only to discover that his lack of information caused him to take the wrong approach.

Here was a situation where the lady had a challenge. She knew what was happening, made a decision and acted it out through jumping up and down.

So many times I have thought about that experience and just smiled outwardly while laughing inwardly. Life holds those experiences for all of us. There is an issue that creates confusion, and you must decide whether to face the issue or just let it exist.

Those really are your only two choices. If you try to stand on the fence, you are actually feeding the confusion. If you decide to do nothing at this time, you are feeding the confusion. You either have to face the issue and resolve or live with it emotionally draining you.

Many don't seem to understand that avoiding anything does not give you breathing space. It actually emotionally chokes you. It doesn't go away; avoiding it just gives it more space in your life. Every time you avoid any issue, you increase the negative presence it has. Every time you choose to let it exist, you strengthen the emotional grip it has on your life. The only freedom is to face it head on and resolve it. You may think that is the more emotionally draining of the choices, but it is not. Yes, it may create an emotional time, but once it is faced, it is over. As long as you let it exist, it stays as a presence gaining emotional momentum. The next time you have to face it you are mentally weaker and it is emotionally stronger.

Confusion is one of the most emotionally paralyzing things you will ever wrestle with. It is an emotional wall your mind cannot see over. Until you make the decision to face it and resolve what is creating it, you are paralyzed and stuck in the Circle of Sameness.

You can get through it, but to achieve this you must ask the right questions and be willing to implement the answers you receive. Asking the right questions means very little if you are not willing to implement the answers.

Here are some questions for you to *honestly* answer:

- *Are there points of confusion in your life you are wrestling with?*

- *Are you better at feeding confusion or resolving issues?*

- *What is the top issue you need to resolve?*

How Do You Know The Right Questions To Ask?

R *reveals an answer, not an opinion*

I *inwardly you are calm with your decision*

G *gathering energy is easy*

H *halts your emotional reacting*

T *there is a clear plan of resolution*

YOU AND YOUR STRESS

*People who work to eliminate stress become
stressful; people learn to control their stress
enhance their creativity.*

Stress? You know what that is, don't you? It
is those days when you feel the walls are caving in.
It is those times when you look around and you
don't know what to touch first. It is those times
where inside you feel out of control.

Stress? You know what it is, don't you? It is
the surge of energy that races through you when
you are excited and nervous at the same time. It is
the emotions you feel when you are close to the
dream you have been stretching to obtain.

Stress! It is not something that comes and
goes in your life. It is an every day, every situation
part of life. Yes, it can be a negative part of your
life. Yes, it can be a positive part of your life.

Stress, like any emotion, has two sides. It
has a positive side that feeds your imagination. It
creates the adrenaline that rushes through you
when the good things are happening and you can't
wait to get to the next part of the journey.

It has a negative side. It is the drain of
energy you feel when you are wrestling with fear,

All negative stress is
the result of you
reacting to a
perception.

uncertainty, worry, doubt or the feeling of being lost and not knowing what you should do.

Many work to deny its presence in their lives, and the more they deny, the stronger the grip it has on their lives. It may sound strange, but it is reality. *People who work to eliminate stress enhance the presence of stress in their lives; people who learn to control the stress in their lives enhance their creativity.*

Stress is and will always be. Stress is anything that makes you uptight. That means it is an ever-present part of your life.

Nita called me, and it didn't take long to feel how out of control her life was. She asked if we could meet to see if there was anything I could do to help her. It happened that I was going to be in her city and had time to visit with her.

When she walked in, her posture told me a lot about her. Her shoulders were drooping and she was walking like someone who was almost out of energy. As she sat down, I looked at her eyes and could see the lack of sleep and the emotional drain that had removed the life from them.

We chatted for a few minutes and I asked her, "What is happening in your life?"

That was all it took for the tears to form and start their journey down her face. She tried to wipe them away, but there were too many of them. "I'm sorry," she said. "I cannot help it. It seems that all I do is cry. I have cried so much I didn't think I had any tears left."

She paused, looked away as she dried her eyes and continued, "I cannot continue to live this way. My life is so out of control. I have nowhere to turn and no one to turn to."

"Let's slow down here. Why don't you tell me what is happening. It is apparent there are some very emotional issues racing inside you."

The major issue was her marriage. She had been married for forty plus years and the relationship had been going downhill for thirty of the forty plus years. She had hung in because of the children. She had put her life on hold in order to make sure the kids had a good life.

I remember her telling me. "I made a big mistake staying for the kids. It cost me thirty years of my life caring about them and now they don't want anything to do with me. He created such a control over their life as kids that today they are easily manipulated by him. They tell me one thing in private and another when he is there. They tell me they respect me as their mother, *but* when their father is ripping me apart, they don't stand up for me. They are so fearful of him they tuck their tails and run away."

"Nita, what would make you happy?"

There was no hesitation in her voice. "What would make me happy is to have my life back. I am so tired of living with all this stress. It has affected me mentally, emotionally and physically. I am having health problems and the doctor tells me it is all related to the stress in my life."

She paused again and I could see her drop into deep thought. "Richard, my business has just disappeared. I am a good salesperson, but I cannot concentrate with all this going on in my life. I get up in the morning with good intentions, *but* they are gone before I even get into the day. I know what I have to do to generate business, but I am just too tired. I go to the office, look at my desk and just fall back in my chair. I cannot get started."

She paused again and I could see her shifting mental gears. "Then, there is my house. I love to clean house, but not now. I cannot stand a messy place, but everywhere I look there are piles and I don't have the energy to face them. I cannot continue to live like this. This has got to stop. I feel trapped; I feel there is no place for me to turn or no place to go. I have to get back to being me."

Another pause and for the first time a little smile appeared on her face. "I don't even know if I know who I am any more. If the real me showed up, I am not sure I would know who that person was. It has been so long since I have felt I was being me. I want that person back."

She paused, the smile left and the tears came back. "I just want my life back. I know what it means, but I don't have the energy to do what needs to be done. Richard, I am tired of being tired; I am tired of not sleeping; I am tired of being made to feel I am not smart; I am tired of being treated like a slave; I am so tired of not living. If this doesn't change, it is going to kill me and I am not ready to die!"

"Nita, do you realize the price tag that may be involved here?"

"Yes! I know what is going to be involved; I understand the war that is going to happen. He is not going to let go without a fight, and the fight is going to be dirty. He is going to do everything he can to hurt me and make me the guilty person. I understand all this, *but* that pain will end. This pain I have been going through is not going to go away until I do something. I am ready, but not looking forward to doing it."

Nita was like so many I meet. Their lives do not belong to them. They are controlled by the people and the things they have given permission to take over and write the script they live each day. Each day she lived that way, she increased the negative stress in her life. Yes, she thought she was doing the right thing. Reality is — as long as she was living in a world that made her react, she was killing herself from the inside out. She was becoming less of a person and more of a prisoner.

Negative stress is the result of reacting. It is your emotional upheaval taking control of your life. It is an inner feeling of darkness where nothing seems to move in actual speed. You feel like you are spinning; you feel almost helpless; you feel like you are standing on the edge of a deep hole and you cannot stop falling. Everything you know seems to have been forgotten. It's just all this pressure weighing on you, and there is no way to get it off your shoulders.

You keep telling yourself:
• *I just want this to be over.*
• *I don't care what it takes; I just want away from this.*
• *I am so stuck and no one seems to care.*
• *I am trapped!*

These perceptions are the result of the negative emotions you are seeing through. There is always an exit door. There is always a way through. There is always an answer.

Slow down; listen to who you are listening to. Slow down; take a deep breath and see everything around you, not just the perceived negatives. Slow down; find someone who is healthy in your life and reach out to them. Working through anything by yourself is your choice. There is always someone there who can help you. You have to get beyond your feeling of guilt and reach out. You have to move beyond your fear of looking weak and realize all humans have stress. All humans will go through the negative moments. Moving forward or staying stuck is a choice you make that is demonstrated through the decisions you act out.

Don't get caught up in the fact that you are feeling stressed. Welcome to being a human. Pay attention to whether you are reacting and increasing the negative stress, or responding and pushing through the event you are facing at this moment. Sound simple? It really *is* simple. Your behavior creates which aspect of stress you have to deal with.

Here are some questions for you to *honestly* answer:

- *Are you better at controlling stress or allowing it to control you?*

- *Is there any aspect of your life that is overwhelming right now?*

- *Are you going to give in to the negative stress?*

What Does It Take To Control Negative Stress?

T *talk to yourself about what is happening*

A *address the reason the stress is increasing*

K *keep all things in perspective*

E *emotionally, slow down*

Notes

YOU AND HONESTY

Most people want honesty as long
as it is not honest.

Most people are not designed to handle honesty. Does that statement surprise you? During my programs I am constantly asking people this question:

Do you always want people to be totally
honest with you?

How do you think most people would answer that question? Think about it for a moment. How would you answer that question? 99.9% answer with a resounding "NO!"

Why? Because most would rather live in the fantasy world. The truth is painful, *but* the reality is — you already know the truth. You just don't want to hear someone say it to you. Many think if they don't hear it, they don't have to do anything about it. The fact is, in already knowing the truth, you have created an internal collision for yourself.

The resistance to hearing the truth is emotional. It is your negative emotions working to keep you trapped in that Circle of Sameness.

As long as you are
running from
the truth,
nothing can
improve.

Those negative emotions are so cunning:

- *They can convince you that hearing the truth is not going to change anything.*

- *Why do that to yourself? Your life is doing just fine.*

- *Hey, everyone needs a fantasy world to live in.*

Reality is — your mind knows the truth and is constantly pushing you to face what *is*. Your mind knows the only way you are going to improve is to face what is, in order to be able to redesign what has been. The process must happen before you can break free of the emotional trap and take your life to the next dimension.

As long as you are denying the truth, nothing can improve. Improvement demands facing what is — with truth.

I was invited to Toronto by a company to see if I would consider spending the year helping them improve their managers. Since I didn't know anything about the company, I scheduled a trip to spend some time doing some interviews and information gathering.

The first two days I was there I talked with a lot of people and watched how the environment operated. It was interesting standing back and watching the inefficiencies and inconsistencies. I wondered why those who were the leaders didn't see what I was seeing. In my interviews with managers it became very evident why neither of these were faced. They were not allowed to. They were told "it would cause more problems than it was worth."

My second evening there I was to have dinner with the CEO, COO and CFO. You knew who they were because they would not tell you their name without telling you their title. Position in this company was very important.

It was a nice restaurant and I was hungry. It had been one of those days that started at 6:30 A.M. and ended an hour before we were to meet for dinner. I had run all day working to gather all my information.

We had small talk at the beginning of dinner and it was polite and somewhat interesting. Just as they placed the entree in front of us, the CEO leaned in, looked at me and said, "So, you have had two days with my people. Tell me what you have learned."

I paused for a moment. My mind was telling me "this is not the place for this conversation" and my stomach was saying "we are not going to get to eat. Forget the conversation; feed me!"

I took a deep breath, looked at him and replied. "You and I have two hours blocked out tomorrow morning, and I would really rather wait to have that conversation when it is just the two of us."

"Why?" came shooting back at me. "I think we can talk about it here. Tell me what you have learned."

I could hear my stomach screaming "Don't do this to me. Feed me!"

"Are you sure you want to involve these two gentleman in this conversation? It might really be better to have it tomorrow morning."

"No, tell me!"

"Well, from the interviews I have done — and watching the happenings in the environment — I think *you* are the problem."

You talk about a table going silent. I thought to myself "you have gone this far; don't stop now."

"You have five years left on your contract and you have already retired. You say with words that you want the company to grow, but then you handcuff your people and won't let them do the things that would really bring improvement to the company environment. They are tired of fighting fires that could be put out; they are frustrated dealing with the same issues over and over. They

95

have lost their desire to do a good job. They don't sense that things are going to improve."

The look on his face told me I was losing my popularity with him. The other two gentlemen at the table were trying to disappear under the table.

"You don't want to hear any problems. You have designed this comfortable life for yourself. Sure, you are still making a profit for your shareholders, but that is soon going to go away. I think you want people to lie to you. See these two men at the table with us? They know what is going on, but they are not going to tell you. If they do, you would probably fire them. You want things to stay the same and have designed the environment to keep it that way."

Well, his redness had reached the tips of his ears and I knew I was in trouble. He took the napkin from his lap, held it tightly in his hand, leaned in and said, "I am not paying you to tell me about me. I am paying you to tell me about my company!"

Before I could stop myself, the words came out. "You are the company. The behavior of your people is consistent with your design. They are what you tell them to be."

That was it for him. He threw his napkin into his plate, stood up and said in a forceful voice. "This dinner is over!"

With that he started across the restaurant. Realizing the other two gentlemen were still sitting at the table staring at their entree they hadn't touched, he turned and said, "I said this dinner is over!"

With that the two guys looked at me and said, "We're sorry." They left the table and followed him out of the restaurant.

It wasn't a surprise to me when he canceled my meeting with him the next morning. I received a message from his assistant telling me his schedule had unexpectedly been rearranged.

I knew what had happened. He wanted honesty as long as it wasn't honest. He wanted me to tell him what he wanted to hear. The truth was not something he was prepared for, nor wanted to hear.

The tragedy is that today the company is gone. It didn't have to happen; it could have been turned around. All that needed to be done was for leadership to face their design with truth and honesty. All the internal issues could have been resolved with just leadership facing what was.

Do you understand how many times this happens in life? It happens in company meetings where people are fearful of expressing their true feelings. Somewhere in the past they have been honest, and were punished for stating the truth. They are not going to go back there. So, what do they do? They play the game of avoiding the process that would resolve and that would allow them to move on. That means what is not faced will be repeated. That simply drains the environment of its positive energy.

It happens in conversations among people in relationships. There is truth that needs to be stated. Their rationalization is "I don't want to hurt them." So, what do they do? They avoid the issue by not stating what needs to be stated. The result is validation of behavior, rather than resolution of an issue. That means things are repeated and the emotional upheaval increases.

The truth may not always be something that is without pain, *but* nothing gets resolved, nothing can improve, nothing can move forward until the truth is put in front of everyone and worked through.

Here are some questions for you to *honestly* answer:

- *Do you want people to always be honest with you?*

- *Are you honest with people when they ask you to be?*

- *Are there issues you need to face with honesty?*

What Does It Take For You To Overcome Your Fear Of Truth?

T *trust must be in place with the people involved*

R *realize you cannot improve without it*

U *underscore the reason it needs to be said*

T *talk it through with the right pace and agenda*

H *have the conversation only when you are calm*

Notes

RESPONDING VS. REACTING
You must respond, not react.

Most people are more emotional than they are logical. When this is realized and reversed, life holds a very different meaning.

A couple of years ago I started a journey with Rachel Torchia and her company, Gateway Title Insurance in Independence, Ohio. In the beginning my mission was to simply sharpen the skills of her leadership partners. Once inside, I realized the journey was going to be much more than that.

Here was an environment where everywhere you turned there was an emotional collision waiting to happen. Service didn't get along with escrow; escrow didn't get along with sales or service; accounting was up in arms with escrow; technical support was screaming at everyone because they were not using the systems correctly.

Then, there was Rachel. She was more than the owner; she was the mother to her group of adopted children called employees. No one was a stranger to Rachel; they all had some form of emotional connection with her. She spent more of her time trying to calm the environment than she

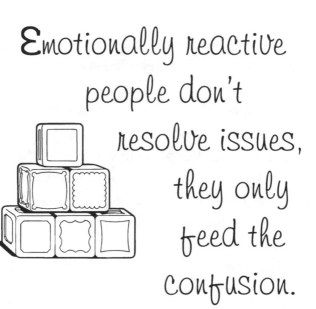

Emotionally reactive people don't resolve issues, they only feed the confusion.

did providing leadership. She was tired, stressed out and not able to be the creative leader she needed to be. Her days were spent fighting the fires that kept erupting inside the walls of the office.

My mission involved helping Rachel see what she had created. Every month when I was in town we started our day with breakfast. This was one time when Rachel was calm and could listen. An environment that is out of control is not an environment where people listen. Their energy is spent reacting emotionally.

I remember our first breakfast together after my initial visit. I knew I had to get her to understand one principle. If she could grasp this one principle, we would have something to build on. If she couldn't, there was no starting point.

"Rachel, there is one thing I need for you to grasp."

She looked at me with a puzzled look and asked, "What's that?"

"It is five words and those five words must be the building block to all we are going to do. Are you ready to hear them?"

"Tell me."

"Okay, here they are. *I must respond, not react.*"

The look on her face told me she didn't really understand what I was saying. "Rachel, there are no words more important to your life than these five. When I look at your company, I see a group of reactionary people running around with their emotions being thrown at each other. No wonder there is so much stress and tension inside those walls."

The picture I painted of her company made her stop and pay attention. "What do we need to do?"

"Rachel, it is simple, but complex. We have to redesign acceptable behavior. We have to make everyone aware of their emotional presence. They have become so used to emotionally attacking each other, they are not even aware they are doing it."

I paused to make sure she was still present in the conversation. "The challenge right now is *you*. You have to become the leader. That means you can no longer treat these people as your adopted children called employees."

"That is not going to be easy. I have a long relationship with most of them. Several of them have been with me from the beginning."

"I know. That is why this is going to be one of the greatest challenges you have ever faced. You are going to have to take the lead by redesigning your relationship with them. You must divorce yourself from being mother and become the leader of your company. At this point your company has no leader. They come to you, not as the owner or leader, *but* because they know you will listen to their problems. That has to stop!"

The look on her face told me this was not what she was wanting to hear. Yet, the light in her eyes told me she understood what I was saying and knew it was right. "How do we start?"

"The first step is to make sure you understand the difference between responding and reacting. I want you to keep track of the times when you see people out of control. I need for you to be able to define the difference to me. I can tell you the difference, but the key is for you to learn to recognize when reacting is controlling the environment. So, for the next month I want you to watch what is happening in your company and keep track of the times you feel things are out of control. Can you do that?"

"I think so!"

That was the beginning of a journey between me and Gateway Title that has lasted over two years now. That may seem like a long time, but for any environment that has been reaction driven to become an environment that is responding takes three to five years. It is not just recognizing what is happening, but facing the people and staying consistent with confronting the reactionary moments. It involves holding people accountable for their behavior and explaining what is acceptable behavior and what is not. It is being willing to let people go who don't want to step up and work to improve.

You have got to respect those few leaders like Rachel, who are willing to take their company, challenge the design they had created, challenge the people to redesign their behavior, stay consistent with the design and move the company forward with a pace it can manage.

Rachel's journey was not without casualties. During the journey she lost several people who were not willing to adapt. They didn't think Rachel was serious about taking the environment from reactionary to responsive. They challenged her as a person and as a leader. A couple had been with her for years and didn't think she would let them go. They didn't understand Rachel's commitment to having a calm workplace where people functioned together as partners, rather than children fighting over their toys.

If you were to visit Gateway Title Insurance Company and ask any one of the people there,

"What is the guiding principle here?," they would answer with five words — *I must respond, not react.*

If you were to visit Gateway Title Insurance Company, you would find a company where issues are handled while they are a concern. The environment is designed to confront, not avoid issues. There is real communication that leads to resolution, not confusion.

As they continue their journey, Gateway Title Insurance Company can become one of those few that become a *great* company. Most companies are average, but say they are great. All you have to do is walk into their environment and feel the emotions that control the interaction among the people. Just listen to the conversations and hear the complaining, the backbiting and discussions about issues that just hang around. These are reactionary environments.

One of the top issues all people face is learning to respond, rather than react. Common behavior reacts, creates a mess and then tries to clean things up. Once the emotional damage has been done, it takes three times the energy to reverse the energy flow.

Do you understand the difference between reacting and responding?

Reacting is the result of your racing in with your emotions guiding all that is happening. Your mind takes a backseat and your emotions define and express your feelings. When your emotions are guiding your presence, the pace speeds up, your listening ability slows down and you are there to make a statement, not resolve issues. The result becomes emotional collisions, unresolved issues and people with hurt feelings. That means there has been no resolution and the issue is still present and still needs to be addressed.

Responding is a design where you walk in with your mind guiding your presence. Your mind is stronger than your emotional feelings. It doesn't mean your emotions are not part of the process; they are just not controlling you. Your emotions are present, but they are secondary to your mental presence.

Where your emotions are about expressing feelings, your mind is about finding a solution. Reacting is not solution-driven; it is about making statements, whether others want to hear them or not. Only when your mind is leading the conversation is there a plan in place to resolve the issue.

Responding is about keeping a calm spirit; it is about creating a pace that everyone can emotionally manage. When you are calm, you are in control. When you are reacting, you are out of control. An out of control person only brings confusion and is unwilling to listen to any conversation about resolving the issue.

Think about this for a minute. Have you ever had a person in your life you couldn't talk to because of how emotional they would become? Have you ever had anyone who always wanted to fight? You couldn't have a calm conversation with them without them going off the wall. These are reactionary people. These are people whose presence makes it impossible to resolve what is in front of you and keeps issues alive and emotionally driven. These people feed confusion, steal the energy of others and are never calm with their lives.

You must respond, not react. This must become one of your foundation principles for your life. Without it you will drag issues from day to day that could be resolved and moved beyond.

Here are some questions for you to *honestly* answer:

- *Are you a reactionary person?*

- *Do your emotions rule your life?*

- *Would responding improve your life?*

How Do You Learn To Respond?

L *listen more, talk less*

E *emotionally slow down*

A *address, don't avoid*

R *revisit, don't relive issues*

N *never take on major issues when you are tired*

YOU AND YOUR DREAM
All human lives collide at the point of agendas.

Have you ever been in a conversation with someone and suddenly realized they were not paying attention to anything you had said, *but* fully expected you to give them your total attention while they were talking? Have you ever had someone put you in the middle of a situation without asking your permission? Have you ever had someone get upset with you because you didn't agree with what they were saying?

If any of the above has happened to you, welcome to the world of agenda collisions. I learned a very valuable lesson while I was on the staff of the church in West Palm Beach:

Human lives collide at the point of agendas,
not issues.

It is the issue that brings people together, but it is the agendas that either resolve the issues or continue the struggle. Most never begin a conversation by establishing the agenda, and without a common agenda there will be no clear communication. The result will be an emotional collision. Walk through a situation that demonstrates what I am talking about.

Without a common agenda, issues simply move in circles and are not resolved.

Have you ever seen an item that you wanted; I mean really wanted; wanted so much you couldn't get it out of your head?

Several years ago, Buick came out with the Riviera Convertible. That was one beautiful car. The Buick dealership was on the main road I had to take home each day. I remember the first time I spotted the car in the showroom. I turned my car around, drove back to the dealership, parked out front and just stared at it on the showroom floor. Each day as I was on my way home, on my way to the office or headed to and from the tennis courts I would slow down and just stare at that car.

I wanted that car! I didn't know what it cost and emotionally I didn't care. I just knew that was the car for me.

This went on for two months. One Friday I was having a conversation with myself. (I do that a lot. I don't know of anyone else who really understands the inside of my head.) I was justifying what I wanted to do the next day. I wanted to play tennis in the morning and then, go buy that Buick Riviera. That would be my Christmas, New Year's and Birthday present to myself. I deserved that car.

Saturday morning I got up, got ready to go play tennis, went into my study, took out my checkbook and wrote out a check to the Buick dealership. On the memo line I wrote for Buick Riviera Convertible. Now, would you say I was a committed buyer?

On the way to the tennis center I stopped by the Buick dealership, parked my car and stared into the showroom. I closed my eyes and could see myself in that car. I remember the goose bumps that raced down my spine. The new blue Buick Riviera convertible was going to be mine.

I don't remember much about my tennis match that morning. All I could think about was that new Buick Riviera convertible.

Chuck, one of the people I regularly played tennis with on Saturday, said to me, "You are not yourself today. Are you okay?"

"Chuck," I said with goose bumps running down my spine, "I am going to buy me a new car today. Not just any new car, *but* a new Buick Riviera convertible."

I drove up in front of that Buick dealership, took my checkbook out of the glove compartment and marched in to buy my new car. I was standing next to the car with my mouth open and the drools running down my chin when Larry arrived. He stood at a distance for a second, approached and said. "Nice car, isn't it?"

"You bet. This is the prettiest car I have ever seen."

"Yes sir, *but* that is not the car for you."

His words awakened me from my vision of driving off in the car. "What?" was my astonished reply. "What did you say?"

"It's a great car, but not the car for you."

Now, I know I didn't look my best. I had been on the tennis court in the Florida sun for three hours, but I didn't look like a bum.

I regained my composure, looked him squarely in the eyes and said, "This is not the car for me. Interesting. Do you have a car you think is for me?"

"Yes, I do. I know just the car for you."

"Please show it to me. I just have to see it."

We walked out of the showroom, out to the back lot, passed most of the cars and ended up at a row of Buick Skylarks. Now, if you know anything about the Buick line of cars, you know you could put the Skylark in the trunk of the Riviera.

He stopped in front of a blue Skylark, pointed to the car with this big salesperson smile and said, "This is the car for you."

"Why do you think this is the car for me?"

"It fits your demeanor."

"My demeanor," I thought to myself. "This little kid doesn't even know me and he thinks he knows my demeanor!"

I took a deep breath to make sure I didn't reach out and kill him right there. I motioned with my finger for him to come close to me. I took out my checkbook, laid it opened on the hood of the little Buick Skylark and asked "Larry, who is this check made out to?"

He looked at the check and replied. "It is made out to the dealership."

Pointing to the memo line I asked him, "Larry, what does it say on this line?"

He read the line, turned bright red and muttered the words on the line — "Buick Riviera Convertible."

"Larry, all I wanted to do today was come here and buy that Buick Riviera Convertible. I wasn't going to haggle you over the price. I just wanted to buy that car."

He took a deep breath, smiled his salesperson smile and said, "And you will look great in that car."

I removed the check from my checkbook, tore my name from the signature line and handed it to him. "I cannot believe you would presume to know me and know what I wanted. You didn't ask me any questions or inquire about what I wanted. You just decided you knew what I should buy."

I could feel my temperature rising, so I slowed down and took a deep breath. "Larry, I wouldn't buy that car from you if you were the last salesperson on this earth. I had dreamed about driving off in that car, *but* you took my dream away from me with this Buick Skylark. Please put this check someplace you can always see it and remember the day you lost the sale of a new Buick Riviera convertible."

With that I turned, walked back to my car, got in and drove off. Later, when I went back and purchased the car, I found out from the sales manager they were having a sales contest on the Buick Skylark. For every one a salesperson sold, they got a $200 spiff.

What an interesting and frustrating experience of agenda collision. I had one agenda, to purchase that blue Buick Riviera Convertible, and Larry had another agenda, to sell me a Buick Skylark so he could receive a $200 spiff.

Most of the complications you face in life will result from the lack of a common agenda. Without a common agenda that everyone is following, conversations will go in circles and not find a resolution.

Most of the disappointments you will experience will result from the lack of a common agenda. When you are seeking to convey a message, and the others don't want to listen because it is not their agenda, you will feel disappointed.

Agendas help everyone understand why this conversation is needed. Agendas keep conversations moving toward a solution.

Agendas slow everything down. A common agenda can help control the emotions that are always part of any conversation about an emotional issue. The faster emotions are moving, the more confusion is created.

A common agenda makes moving forward possible. Anything that is not moving forward is moving in a circle that will keep emotions running high and resolution impossible. Common agendas allow for completion, clear communication and the resolution of issues.

Here are some questions for you to *honestly* answer:

- *Are you good at establishing a common agenda?*
- *Are there issues right now you need to resolve?*
- *Do you understand the need for an agenda?*

How Do You Establish An Agenda?

A *a desire to resolve must be in place*

G *getting clear of purpose is a must*

E *emotions must be put aside*

N *no detours allowed*

D *direction must be established*

A *a calm pace is critical*

Notes

YOU AND YOUR PROBLEMS

YOU AND YOUR PROBLEMS

A problem is a concern you didn't address yesterday.

Some day you should slow down and listen to how many times people use the word "problem." It will amaze you. It is one of the most used words in the English language. What many don't seem to realize is the effect the word has on your life.

Think about it! What does the word "problem" denote?

- *Something is wrong.*
- *Something you don't want to face.*
- *Something that requires confrontation.*
- *A conversation with another you may not want.*
- *Something you will more than likely avoid.*

Are any of those really positive? Each is designed for the issue to continue; not to be resolved. Each is designed to steal energy from you, rather than add energy to your life.

What happens to you when you live avoiding an issue? You worry about having to take care of it. The emotional drain this creates causes you to procrastinate because *now is never a good time to do this.*

121

A problem always
gives birth to
more
problems.

You are uncomfortable being around the person(s) involved in the event. Any time you are around them you are fearful the issue is going to come up. If you talk to them, it is a guarded conversation. You don't want to get into it with them. You are not ready to have this conversation.

The issue doesn't go away. It continues to play in your mind. Your mind is such an interesting part of your life. It is there to resolve issues and make sure you don't have problems. It keeps a list of all the things you are avoiding. Anytime it has a chance to remind you of what you are doing, it is more than happy to do so. This means there is no freedom from the event until it has been faced and resolved.

Here are a couple of thoughts you need to think through: First, a problem is always about yesterday. A concern is about today. Think about this!

Problems keep you facing yesterday. They don't allow you to focus on today; they keep you staring at yesterday. The more you stare at yesterday, the less energy you have for the events of today. Do you realize the ramifications of this?

You have designed your life to drag this issue with you wherever you go. That means a constant drain that doesn't allow you to replenish your life with positive energy.

You cannot stay focused on anything you do. Problems always call attention to themselves. You don't have to stop and think about it being present. It will manifest itself in the everyday of your life. It is there and will remind you of that fact.

Here is another thought you need to think through: A problem always gives birth to more problems. That is not a pleasant thought.

I have found in working with people that anyone who has a problem, has problem_s. You cannot have just one problem. The avoidance of one problem creates a series of problems that just keep multiplying. That means a problem can create a lifestyle of problems.

Think about this. It means even if you can avoid one problem, there is another aspect of it you have to stare at. That is exhausting just to think about.

The difference between a problem and a concern is about personal trust. Does that statement take you by surprise? People who have problems lack the personal trust necessary to face the situation. When you trust yourself, you address anything that can take your life in the wrong direction.

The difference between a problem and a concern is about controlling your fear. Most don't address the issue at the level of concern, because they are fearful of what might happen. They live with this unrealistic idea that if they leave it alone, it will take care of itself. Reality is — it doesn't! It keeps attaching more negative emotions and just keeps redefining itself through more problems.

The difference between a problem and a concern involves stating the truth. It is amazing how many problems exist because one cannot admit they are wrong. It is easier to find fault, place blame or deny personal responsibility. Until truth prevails, there will be problems.

Addressing any issue at the time of concern allows you to do so with calmness. Concerns don't have too many emotions tangled up in them. The greater the time and distance between the issue and addressing it, the more emotions the situation will attract. The greater the emotional entanglement, the greater the challenge of facing it.

Addressing any issue at the time of concern allows you to do so with clarity. When you are calm and clear, you are in control of the flow of what is happening. As your emotions take over, your mind is pushed aside. That means forgetting what you know to be right. As you lose your clarity, uncertainty increases. Uncertainty paralyzes you, which results in procrastination.

Addressing any issue at the time of concern allows you to focus on the "now," rather than having to wrestle with yesterday. Tragic, but true. Most people are designed to repeat yesterday, not live today. That happens because you don't face the moments in which you are living. Something that could be resolved without much emotional entanglement is pushed aside. Each time you push it aside you change the design of the situation. Each time it is redesigned it takes on a bigger emotional presence. The bigger the presence, the greater the fear of facing it. Problems really can take on a life of their own.

Mary has to be the #1 Problem Person I have ever met. Her appearance in my life was both a curse and a blessing. She came to me because one of her friends recommended me.

I remember the call I got from the friend. "Richard, I hope you aren't going to be mad at me."

Now, that is an unusual way to start a conversation. You just know what is to follow is not going to be the best news you have ever had. "What do you mean?" was my reply.

"I have asked a friend of mine to give you a call. Her life is a giant dark hole she seems to be slipping deeper and deeper into. She needs someone who will be straightforward with her, and you are that person. Please see if you can help her."

It wasn't long after she called that my phone rang, and it was Mary. When I answered the phone, these were the words I was greeted with. "Hi! I am the problem person Susan said was going to call you. I hope I am not bothering you."

That began a journey filled with lessons for both of us. In all my years of working with human behavior I have never, and I mean never, met a person so problem-driven as Mary. During just one conversation we had, she used the word "problem" 64 times in a matter of two hours. This was the word she used to describe her life.

Every aspect of her life was a problem:
• There were problems at work. No one liked her; the job was too difficult; the hours didn't fit her scheduled needs; she couldn't quit because they had to have the money.
• There were problems at home. The kids were

driving her crazy; her husband never came home; the house was too small; the neighborhood was not good for raising children; she had no friends there, and the more she tried to make friends, the more she got the cold shoulder.

• There were problems in her personal life. With all she had to do, there was no time for her; her husband was too demanding of her time; the kids required too much from her; she didn't have time to do anything she wanted to do; no one seemed to care about her; she was just a puppet that they enjoyed making dance around their needs.

You couldn't talk to her about any aspect of her life. Her favorite line was "it does no good to talk about all this stuff. It will never go away. My life will be a problem until I die."

One day I posed a question that really made her angry at me. "Mary, do you enjoy having all these problems in your life? I get the feeling they give you both a reason to live and a reason to complain."

Well, that didn't set well with her. "Enjoy them! They are going to be the death of me. If I enjoyed them, why would I be here talking to you about my life? What do you think I am — a masochist?"

"Yes, Mary I believe you are. You use your

problems to get attention. If you didn't have all these self-induced problems, you wouldn't have a reason to live. You thrive on them."

The look on her face expressed the anger that was racing through her. "I cannot believe you are saying this to me. You are supposed to be here to help me, not put me down. Who do you think you are talking to me like this?"

"Mary," I said as calmly as I could. "You are here because I agreed to listen to you. That doesn't mean I have to agree with your analysis of the situation. I have taped the conversations we have had. Would you like to listen to yourself?"

I paused, she looked at me with daggers flying and said. "No, I don't want to listen to the tapes!"

"Mary, I agreed to see you to offer you help. You don't want help; you want me to agree with you and I cannot do that. There is not an issue in your life you cannot solve *if* you are willing to face it. You are the problem, *not* the people around you. You create what is, and then feast on it."

It will probably come as no surprise to you, *but* that was the last time I saw Mary. She called back the next day and canceled her remaining appointments with me.

Issues, things and people in your life are not

the problem. *You are!* You choose what every event is going to mean to your life. If you choose to face it while it is a concern, you keep your life problem free. If you choose to avoid it while it is a concern, you make sure your tomorrow will be driven by problems. Interesting! It all boils down to what you choose to do with the events your life is handed.

Here are some questions for you to *honestly* answer:

- *Are you good at addressing issues while they are concerns?*

- *Do you keep problems in your life because you need them?*

- *Can you see your life problem free?*

How Do You Address Issues While They Are A Concern?

C *create a solution environment*
O *open yourself to confrontation*
N *negative opinions are not acceptable*
C *communicate your true feelings*
E *examine your emotions about what is*
R *relax with what you are facing*
N *never let tomorrow become the answer room*

You and Your Stamina

Passion and stamina are twins.

A few years ago I did a piece of research designed to help me understand what happens to us mentally and emotionally as we get older. It was interesting because it revealed three things to me.

I learned that the older you get mentally and emotionally *the more stubborn you become.* Have you ever been around a stubborn person? The more set they become in their ways, the less willing they are to listen. They don't accept anything they don't agree with. It is like having a conversation with Archie Bunker. There is one way of thinking and that is his way.

Stubborn people create a real sense of frustration for those around their life. They drain others and leave them feeling unimportant. For most people the older they get the greater their stubbornness.

I learned the older you get mentally and emotionally *the more resistant you are to change.* Now, you know change is not attractive to most at any age, but the older you get, the bigger the issue of change becomes. Why?

One reason is that the aging process makes

131

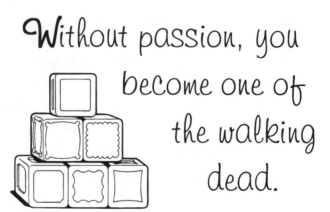

Without passion, you become one of the walking dead.

us more conservative. When you were young, you would take the risk. You had a dream and the dream was important. To achieve that dream you had to step out of your comfort zone. That wasn't always fun, *but* what the heck. You wanted the dream, so you stretched for it. Then, as you get older, that reverses itself. You are no longer willing to risk; you don't think as creatively; your decisions are not filled with stepping into the unknown. Your behavior becomes conservative and leads to the second reason you become a bigger fighter of change.

The aging process makes you want to protect what you have. Hey, would you want to lose everything you have obtained and have to start over with nothing? When I ask that question, the majority answer with a resounding "NO!" What happens when you start protecting what you have? You lose your creative edge. Have you ever known a person who, when they were growing, trusted their inner feelings and would step into the unknown in order to achieve their dream?

How important is creative thinking? It is what keeps you mentally alive and positioned to see the new possibilities in life. When you stop thinking creatively, and start working to protect what you have, you lose your edge. The other side of this is when you become conservative, you also start giving up on life. Many people start their dying cycle when they stop living with a creative spirit. The mind needs challenges to remain young.

The third thing I learned was the older you get mentally and emotionally *the less stamina you have.* I can hear some of your minds as you read this saying, "Richard, as your body gets older, you get tired quicker."

Let me tell you about Art. Art was 72 years young when I met him. When I was in college at East Central University, I played on the tennis team. I would stay after practice and work on my serve. At about 5:30, Art would show up. We would always hit the ball together for about and hour. No, he couldn't move as fast as a young kid, but he didn't need to. He would make you do all the running. You could put a tennis ball can on the court and tell Art "hit the can." Know what? He could do it.

One day Art and I were standing at the net talking and I ask him the question I had wanted to ask for some time. "Art, you are 72, but you are not old. So many people your age are old. What makes you different?"

He got this big smile on his face, looked me squarely in the eyes and said. "I don't want to be old. Yes, I know my body isn't what it use to be, but my mind is as sharp or sharper than it has ever been."

He paused, looked around, fell into a deep thought and continued talking like I wasn't even there. "I have watched so many of my friends die because they didn't have any purpose for their life. They got old because they just lost their passion for life. I still have my passion; there are still things I want to learn; there are a few places I want to see. I am not ready to die."

I have never — and hope I never — forget his words. "I still have my passion for life." Art taught me a very valuable lesson. Stamina and passion are twins. As long as you have your passion for life, you will have the stamina necessary to live. *If* and when you lose your passion for life, you lose your stamina.

Stamina is the inner resolve to fight for what you want. Stamina is the inner strength that finds meaning in the situations your life is handed. Stamina keeps you focused when things around you may appear a little blurry.

The great challenge many face today at all ages is passion. When your passion is weak, it becomes easy to walk away. When your passion is gone, you are no longer mentally and emotionally present. When there is no passion, there is no purpose.

Passion is what lights our inner fire. Passion is what keeps you pushing forward when you aren't sure of the trail. Passion is what creates your love affair with life. Passion is created by living your dream.

That may be the real issue! Most aren't living their dream; they have settled for the moment.

This is true with so many marriages I see. Some get married because they want someone in their life. They cannot stand to be alone. They really aren't passionate about that person; they have settled.

So many who get married lose their passion for their mate. When they get married, they stop dating. Dating is the most important ingredient in marriage to keep the passion alive. Dating is a time of sharing; it is a time of feeling important to the other person. Dating brings meaning to the entire relationship.

I watch it with people who go to work each day. They are not passionate about what they are doing. It is just a job. They show up to get a paycheck. They would be a lot happier if they got a check for staying home. We do have several in this country that do that.

When you lose your passion for any area of your life, you lose your stamina. You find yourself tired all the time. Not really from the energy you are expending, *but* because you are not having fun. It is *fun* that keeps refilling your inner energy well. If there is no fun, the well runs dry. That means the stamina is gone.

One night I was having dinner with some friends of mine and their daughter was with us. She was graduating from college the next week and already had a job. Now, this job was going to pay her $55,000 to start and she had no experience.

I asked her this question. "Are you excited about your new job?"

She didn't look up. She just said. "It's okay. It's a job."

"How many in your graduating class already have a job?"

"I don't know. I don't think it is very many. Many of my friends are depressed because they don't know what they are going to do."

"That is so true with so many who are graduating today. I have known several who went months without being able to find a job. Not you! You have a job that is going to train you and pay you very well while the training is happening. Isn't that great?"

"I guess so," she replied in a less than energetic tone.

I could see the look on her parents' face. Later when it was just her parents and me, her dad looked at me and said. "I don't get it. She should be jumping up and down with joy. She has a job and is being paid more than she is worth. I don't understand why she isn't elated."

If you understood their family, you would understand why she wasn't happy. Her dad had spent his entire working career doing something he didn't want to do. He started very young and worked his way up to a top management position. The pay was great and he was trapped.

During one of the conversations I had with him, I asked him "Why are you still doing what you are doing?"

He stared at me with an amazed look on his face and said. "What else would I do? I am 53 and this is all I have done. Where would I go? No one wants to hire a has-been. I've just got to hang in here a little while longer and I can retire. When that happens, my life will begin."

Now, do you understand where his daughter got her job understanding from? He has no passion for what he is doing with his life. He goes each day and puts in his day. He comes home and brings his tired spirit to the family. He is among the million who make up the walking dead.

These people are simply existing in their shell called a body. They have very little energy in their life. They exist in a world where they feel very little, have few things to be excited about and are hoping to win the lottery so they can start living.

If these people have any enjoyment, it is thinking about tomorrow. Today is just another day in the prison called life. No wonder they are tired, exhausted and feel trapped. They are!

Passion is the key to stamina. Now, I am not saying you won't get tired. You will, *but* there is a difference between being tired and being exhausted. I get asked all the time "Don't you get tired with all the traveling you do?" The answer is "*Yes*!" The difference is I don't get exhausted.

Tiredness is the natural result of using energy to achieve something, but because there is passion for what you are doing, you are recapturing the energy you are expending. Your passion creates the joy and the joy brings energy back.

Exhaustion is the result of expending energy and having nothing to replenish it. You are expending and not refilling. That will leave you with less and less reserves to draw from. Over a period of time you have nothing left to give. The result is that you show up and walk through a day without purpose and without power. You are the walking dead.

Here are a some questions for you to *honestly* answer:

• *Do you enjoy the business part of your life?*

• *Are you still passionate about your life?*

• *What would you do differently with your life if you weren't afraid?*

How Do You Keep Passion Alive?

P *plan your dream*

A *align yourself with growing people*

S *stay centered on your dream*

S *seek new opportunities*

I *invest in your mind*

O *open yourself to taking risk*

N *never settle*

YOU AND YOUR BEHAVIOR
Your behavior never lies.

Life is not defined by what you say, *but* by
the behavior you use to either deny or confirm
what you have said. This is what creates your
presence. The sooner you realize this fact, the less
confusion you will have in your life and the less
confusion you will create for others. Linda defined
this with the story she brought to my life.

"I really need your help!" were her words as
she approached me. "You were talking to me
today."

She paused to see if I would let her continue.
I stopped packing my projector, motioned to her to
sit down, and leaned back to listen.

"I hope I am not intruding, but I have never
had anyone look at me and know exactly where I
was. Let me tell you a little about my situation. My
husband and I own a sales company. When we
started it, he was driven to make it succeed. It took
three years, and he made it the #1 real estate
company in our town. Once he had achieved that,
it seemed he just lost interest. Now, his presence in
the company creates so much confusion."

She paused, so I jumped in. "How does he

All behavior has an agenda.

create the confusion you are talking about?"

"He never carries through. He will tell people he will do things and then, he never carries through. I have been covering for him. I tell people he is just busy, and it slipped his mind. That worked for a while, *but* when it becomes consistent behavior, people know what I am doing."

She paused, so I asked her, "Have you tried talking to him?"

The look on her face said this was a sore point. "Try talking to him! I have talked to him until I am talked out. I have tried to explain to him what he is doing. I have tried to show him how he is losing credibility with the people. Several of our salespeople have talked to him to see if there is something wrong. There is no talking to him."

She paused long enough to let her emotions settle. "He just gets this indignant look on his face and either clams up or walks away. I don't know what to do. Recently, we lost two of our best people. They came to me and told me they just couldn't put up with his inconsistency any more. They were tired of being "lied" to by him. I asked them to talk to him, but they didn't want to. I told Stephen they were leaving, and he just shrugged his shoulders. I asked him to go talk to them, and he didn't want to. I finally told him what they had said and it made him mad. He got red and said, if that is what they think, they don't need to be here. That was the breaking point for me. I can't live with this anymore."

Again she paused to regain her composure. "Richard, when you said behavior never lies, I knew right then something had to be done. The other day, I tried to talk to him about his behavior in the company — and he got really angry with me and said this is the way I am. You and everyone just better get used to it. That really hurt. It made me feel he just doesn't care about what he is doing to the company anymore."

That conversation started a two year journey with their company. It didn't take long inside the company to feel the impact of Stephen's presence. His inconsistency made everything he said a joke to the people. It not only affected his presence with the people, but also the presence of his leadership partners. There were many points of confusion created by his behavior. His behavior became the topic of conversation with the people, not selling. This didn't help Stephen's presence. He would chastise the people for not selling. It got so bad that people didn't want to go to the sales meetings.

Their words to me were "Why should I go

listen to him rant and rave about what *I* am not doing, when he didn't do what he said *he* was going to do. What right does he have to criticize me?"

The most intense conversations I had were with him. He was not an easy person to talk to. When he didn't want to talk, he would withdraw into his world of silence. He knew what he was doing. For years, that had become his way of avoiding issues. Even though he would acknowledge that this was something that needed to be addressed, his behavior said he wasn't going to talk.

He was a classic example of a person in a people position who was not a people person. He was the most content when he could close the door to his office and shut the world out. The only time he wanted to talk was when something was not the way he thought it should be. Then, he would speak in an angry voice that just pushed his people further away. He would tell them about his concern and then, his behavior would contradict his words.

It took almost 18 months to get him to face his behavior. It took over a year for him to understand the wisdom of *behavior never lies*. It took months for him to accept what his presence was doing to his company. Today, if you were to

145

visit their company, you would find a very calm and consistent environment. Their company is back to growing, rather than being paralyzed by Stephen's behavior. Stephen is much more aware of what his presence brings to the environment. He realizes his behavior can either take the company forward or create a level of confusion that stops people in their tracks.

There is such a strong message wrapped up in these three words — *behavior never lies*. When you first meet someone, you normally take them at their word. Over a period of time, you will start watching the connection between their words and their behavior. If there are consistent inconsistencies, you start questioning whether they mean what they say. If the consistent inconsistencies continue, you stop believing what they are telling you. The result is that you stop listening to them. When that happens, nothing gets better. Without being able to trust the words of a person, you become skeptical of what they are saying.

Behavior becomes the defining point you use with people. Respect, listening, trust and the desire to be around them are just a few of the things that are affected by the inconsistency between their words and their behavior.

Behavior becomes the visual aspect used to define who you really are. Behavior defines how much you can trust them. When there are inconsistencies between the spoken word and the acting out of the words through behavior, negative emotions are created by those who are watching more than they are listening.

Behavior states your true agenda. All behavior has an agenda. Where words may say one thing, behavior presents what a person really is about. If you really want to know the intentions of a person, study their behavior. It will never lie about their real agenda.

Behavior shows the ethics of a person. If a person's word is not their bond, there is not much you trust about them.

The reality is — behavior never lies!

Here are some questions for you to *honestly* answer:

- *Does your behavior present any contradictions?*

- *Does your behavior make people doubt you?*

- *Can people trust you to do what you say?*

147

Your Behavior Defines Truth When:

T *there is consistency*

R *results happen*

U *unravels the confusion*

T *there is an agenda*

H *holds you accountable*

YOUR #1 QUEST

The #1 thing a human life wants to know is that they matter.

I have never met a person who didn't want to feel noticed. I have never met a person who didn't want to feel valuable. *Yet*, one of the most common challenges I dealt with in the counseling room was people who didn't feel their presence made a difference. They felt like outsiders in their home and in their job. This made them question their self worth.

As much as it may sound trite, the #1 thing a human wants to know is that they matter. It is a quest that can calm a person down or send them off the deep end. It is a longing that can make a person feel loved or make them feel unloved. It is one of the most critical unspoken desires of people.

I remember one counseling session I was doing with this couple that had been married for thirty five years. They had grown comfortable with each other and it would be an understatement to say the magic of romance was gone.

They were both in my office. She was crying and crying. He was just sitting there not

149

Words mean
nothing without
the action that
makes them
come alive.

saying a word. She looked at him, wiped her eyes
and said to me. "He never tells me he loves me
anymore."

Well, that was all he could take. He stood
up, walked across the room, turned, looked at her
and said. "I come home every night, don't I?"

In his mind his coming home should have
been enough, *but* she needed more. Just being
around another person doesn't necessarily tell
them how you feel. They need to hear with their
eyes and their ears that they are important. Without
that, their inner spirit will question their place.

*The #1 thing a human wants to know is that
they matter.*

I had this recently painted again in my life
with my work with Jack and Mary. They have been
married for twenty years and have four great kids.
Jack is a workaholic. Yes, his business is time
consuming. Yes, his business demands a lot of his
attention. Yes, there is stress on him.

These are all the things he keeps reminding
Mary about. There is no question that Jack loves
Mary very much. He has never really thought
about his life without her.

The first time I talked to Mary alone, the
smile that is always on her face disappeared and
was replaced by the tears. She sat there looking at

me. I could tell there were things she wanted to say, but didn't know how to say them or where to start.

Finally, she took a deep breath and started. "I don't know how much more I can take. I love Jack more than anything, *but* he is driving me away."

Her pause told me she was hurting inside and needed to gather herself before she continued. "He never pays any attention to me. He comes home late, eats supper and never says a word. Then, he gets up and goes to his office and works. If I go in there, he lets me know he needs to concentrate. Concentrate! I think he is just avoiding spending time with me."

Her faced turned red and I could feel the anger that was present. "Now, he is even ignoring the kids. Our oldest son begs for his father's time and he just doesn't seem to get it. I am watching as he chases him away with his lack of attention. I am an adult and can handle it, *but* he is a child wanting his father's attention and can't get it."

Her face changed and her voice got louder. "I won't let him do that to the kids. They don't deserve this. He is their father and they need time with him. If they are not important, then there is no reason for any of us to be here."

"What am I supposed to do?" was the question she posed with tears streaming down her face. "I am at my wits end. I love him with all my heart, *but* it hurts when he ignores me. There are times when I want to grab something and just hit him."

When she paused, I asked, "Have you tried talking to him about this?"

"Talk to Jack!" she said in a very indignant tone. "You don't talk to Jack. If he doesn't want to listen, he just tunes you out or walks away."

She paused and gathered herself. "Do you know why I work at the office? It is not because I enjoy working there. I go there because I can be around him. I see him more there than when we are at home."

She stared into the distance, wiped the tears from her face, looked at me with a questioning look and said. "Sick, isn't it? I really don't know what to do. I don't want to lose him, but I can't continue the way things are. Do you think there is any possibility he can change?"

When I had the opportunity to talk to Jack, I had several questions I wanted to ask him.

"Jack," I said, "How are things at home?"

The look on his face said he was surprised by my question. "Okay! I guess."

"What do you mean you guess?"

"Well, Mary and I don't talk much unless it is about the kids. With them, there is always something to talk about. If they are not into one thing, they are getting into something else."

"Jack, do you love Mary?"

He looked at me again with this puzzled look on his face. "Of course I love her."

"Are you *in* love with her?"

"Yes, I am in love with her. Why are you asking? Do you think I don't love her?"

"No, I think you love her. You would be crazy if you didn't. She is one of the neatest women I have ever met. I know she is in love with you, *but* Jack, she is very lonely."

That statement took him by surprise. "What do you mean she is lonely? Her life is always busy. She always has something going on. She is busy with the kids. She is busy with her mother. She is busy with what she does at home and at work. How could she be lonely?"

"Well, just listen to what you just said. She is busy with kids, mother, home and work. Nowhere in there did you put yourself. Jack, what she is lonely for is *you*. Why do you think she fills her life with so many different things?"

There was this blank look on his face.

"Jack, when was the last time you took Mary on a date? I mean just the two of you out for an evening?"

"I asked her if she wanted to go out. When I went to the business conference recently, I asked her to go and she said she couldn't because of the kids."

"Now, listen to what you just said. You asked her if she wanted to go out. You asked her if she wanted to go to a business conference with you. Jack, you need to stop asking her if she wants to go out. You need to plan the evening and take her out. You need to take her on a date."

"Richard, she won't do it because of the kids."

"Jack, that's her excuse. She is wanting you to take the lead. At work you are the leader. You direct the people and things get done. Then, you go home and you sit down for dinner and then you disappear into your study. You don't really live there with your family; you hang out there. And, asking her to go to a business conference is asking her to go to the one thing she sees that takes you away from her. You need to slow down and pay attention to what you are saying, doing and expecting."

I paused long enough to make sure he was

with me. "Jack, what Mary needs to know is that she matters to your life. You say you love her, and I know you do. You have just forgotten how to be her mate and her lover. I know you tell her you love her, but that isn't good enough. She needs to feel your love. Words mean nothing without the action that makes them come alive. You have got to take the lead in your relationship. She is so tired of begging for your attention. Your kids even question whether you love them or not. You are present in the house, but you are not present in their lives. There is a big difference, and that difference is how people define whether they feel they matter to you. You need to wake up and see what you are doing, before you wake up and everyone is gone."

Since that conversation, Jack has been striving to make the necessary improvements. It has been a real challenge for him. You don't redesign behaviors you have been living for a while overnight. He and Mary have gone on a few dates that Jack has planned. He spends less time at work and more time at home with the family.

The last time I visited with Mary she said to me, "Jack is really trying. I can see a difference in him. I can also tell this is not easy on him. Oh, not because he doesn't want to be with us, but because he has not been there in the past. The kids are noticing too. They look forward to him coming home. I just hope he doesn't slip backward. That would kill them."

I know it would kill her also. She was skeptical about Jack, but was liking what he was doing. It will take them time to get back to being a family. It will take time for Jack and Mary to get their relationship back on track, *but* the good news is that they are working on it. That is more than a lot of couples. It is so challenging to turn a relationship around, once you have started the process of being strangers. Two people can share a house, sleep in the same bed, create and have a child and still be strangers.

Reality is — it all goes back to not knowing that you matter. Most would blame it on the lack of communication. The breakdown in communication is always going to happen when people lose contact with each other. The loss of contact happens when people no longer feel valuable to the relationship they are in.

When they don't feel they matter, they go away. Some do it through divorce; some just withdraw into their own world; some lose themselves in activities. It doesn't matter how they do it; the result is the breakdown of a life.

Here are some questions for you to *honestly* answer:

- *Do the important people in your life know they matter to you?*

- *What do you do to let them know their importance to you?*

- *Is your life too busy to give them quality time?*

What Tells A Person They Matter To You?

P *personal attention*

E *energy that you present*

R *really being there when you are there*

S *surprises that create emotional hugs*

O *opening your eyes and ears to them*

N *noticing them in many different ways*

YOU AND YOUR DREAM

A life without a dream is a life with an empty internal reservoir.

Have you ever had someone tell you that you have to have goals to succeed in life? I don't agree with that statement. In fact, I have found goal setting to be one of the most negative teachings many have been taught.

Now, don't read more into this than I am saying. I am not saying goals don't have a place. There is a place for goals, *but* not as the end-all for all you want to achieve. Statements you write don't have power unless there is a direction you are pointing them toward. Unless your goals are connected to your imagination, they become a fantasy that will exhaust you.

Two of my favorite people I have ever had enter my life are Ted and Nancy Gehrig. I met Ted at a Quixtar meeting in Ft. Lauderdale, and that conversation began a year of working together through my Private Coaching Program. I remember the first time I visited their home for our meeting. I was noticing all the surroundings when I was captured by their refrigerator door. There, taped to the door, were all these pictures of things. The centerpiece was this very large and beautiful house.

159

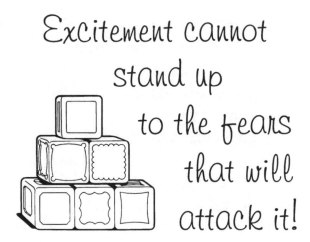

Excitement cannot
stand up
to the fears
that will
attack it!

My question was simple. "What are these pictures about?"

Ted looked at them, turned to me and said. "Those are our goals. Each one is a goal we are wanting to reach."

"How are you going to reach them?"

"Action! You have to take the right action."

I pointed to the house and asked, "What action will get you this one?"

"We have to work hard and stay focused."

Ted could tell by the look in my eyes that this was the wrong answer. "Ted, I have seen a lot of people fill their lives with pictures of things they want. I have even watched many of them work very hard *and* never get them. It is not about having a picture that represents a goal you have. It is about having a dream that fills your imagination with energy, persistency, belief and behavior designed to create the belief."

At that moment neither one of them understood what I was talking about. They have come from a world where they had been taught that having goals was all you needed. There is nothing further from the truth.

So many I have worked with have had goals, *but* still fell short of what they were striving to achieve. Goals in and of themselves are not the answer. Words written on a paper that you stare at carry more frustrations than they do personal power. These things called goals must have a connection point to the creative process of your life. Without the connection point, your goals become vulnerable to the negative moments of life.

How many times have you and I watched a person get excited by the moment they are handed, start a journey that becomes a moment and end up frustrated with what they have done? Do you understand that is the majority of people. *Why*? The answer is simple and complex.

You start with excitement that never matures into enthusiasm. Excitement is what captures us emotionally. We see something and think that's the answer we have been looking for. You create an emotional happening and even write what you want to achieve. Then, without the proper mental diet, it dies before it ever comes to full life.

Excitement is driven by the external factors. As those external factors change, so does the energy. Excitement cannot stand up to the fears that will attack it. Excitement cannot stand up to the disappointments that will happen. Staring at goals will not give you the internal power to work through the confusion that comes with every journey. Excitement is an external cord looking for an internal source of power. Goals cannot supply the power.

Enthusiasm is driven by the internal connection points. Its source of power is the inner desire created by the possibilities your imagination keeps designing and redesigning. It is the mental picture that allows you to see beyond the frustrations with what is not happening; it is the mental picture that allows your desire to remain stronger than your fear; it is the mental picture filled with the colors of possibility that allows you to see through the gray sky confusion paints.

Your imagination is not about writing goals; it is about creating a dream! Goals are more emotional than they are mental. Dreams are more mental than they are emotional. This is not to say they are not both important; they are. You just must realize which one comes first. Goals without the internal connection point of the dream become wasted energy. Dreams become the internal energy plugs that the goals plug into. The dream is the big picture. It is the energy source of the journey. The goals become the baby steps to getting there.

You don't just visualize a dream and wave the magic wand and it happens. You have to create the blueprint and then institute the steps that bring structure to what you are striving to achieve.

Most give up, because they are driven by creating moments, not a journey. Then, when what they want doesn't happen overnight, they give up. They have listened to some motivational guru tell them "Just do it!" The challenge is that it is not about "just doing it"; it is about continuing to strive to achieve it.

Not achieving your stated desire is not as much about not having the talent as it is about not having the patience and willingness to invest the time. It is about not being willing to seek the insights and implement them into a journey.

A life that is built on moments is a life that will be filled with disappointments, trapped in the Circle of Sameness and characterized by starting things it never completes.

The key is being able to answer three questions:

- *What do I really want?*
- *Why do I really want it?*
- *What price am I really willing to pay to achieve it?*

These three questions are the key to designing a journey guided by a dream. These three questions are the key to having the consistent persistency to stay focused through the moments of doubt. These three questions are the key to having the persistent consistency to stay focused when it seems that everything is going wrong. These three questions are about creating the stability to complete what you have stated you want.

The first question — *what do you really want?* — is about finding a direction. Too many get a notion and start without really sensing if this is the direction they should be going. Before you start any journey, you must be sure you are on the right road.

Excitement is not enough to carry you through. There must be more! There must be the belief that your talents will allow you to achieve the desired result. Anytime you get into a process where you don't have the talent required, you are feeding your fears and not your dream. At some point the fear will kill the dream, and you will be left with another disappointment to store in your vault of negative reasons.

Excitement is not enough! There must be a support group that you can trust will be there for you. Just because someone tells you "go for it" doesn't mean they will be there when you need a shoulder. Most of the time these will be the same people that look at you and tell you "I told you so" when things are upside down.

You need traveling companions. These are people who are walking the journey, not talking about what it can do for you. These are people who can share victories, not stories. These are people who can listen without having to tell you a war story. These are people who are living their dream and understand the meaning and power that brings.

Excitement is not enough to carry you through! You have to have a clear picture of what you are working toward. Direction is critical to sustaining energy. Without direction you will feel lost in the jungle of confusing roads. Many roads will look like the right direction, *but* many are dead ends. You must be traveling at a pace that allows you to see all the road signs. There are always the road signs, but if you are moving too fast, you will miss them.

The second question — *why do you really want it?* — is about discipline. This is another aspect of the journey that will make or break you. Discipline is about the consistent persistency needed to have the persistent consistency to continue when you are traveling through the valleys of the unknown and uncertain.

Discipline is about having a strong foundation of self trust. Too many people talk to hear themselves talk, not to define what they are really working to achieve. Too many fill their paragraphs of words with negative thoughts, rather than positive understandings. To achieve any challenge in your life you need to trust in your ability to do it. When you fill your journey with doubt and worry, uncertainty will take over and crack the foundation of trust necessary to make it through the dark moments.

Discipline is about being able to stay focused. This is one of those consistent challenges for most people. They start with the excitement, not realizing the excitement can only take them so far. When they reach the end of that road, they feel lost and uncertain. Without realizing it, they start staring at the struggles and lose their focus on the journey. When you lose your focus, you weaken your inner resolve. This causes you to have some very interesting conversations with yourself. Conversations about:

• *How could I ever believe this could be?*
• *How could I have gotten sucked into this again?*
• *I am a loser and will always be a loser.*
• *I should just stick to the way I have always been.*

Each of these is the "Old" you working to drag you back to yesterday. Yesterday is not about your dream; it is about stories of justification, reasons and lies.

The only thing that will keep you working on improving today is staying focused on what needs to be done *now* to keep you moving forward. That demands discipline.

The third question — *what price am I really willing to pay to achieve this?* — is about your desire. The critical issue here is how far are you willing to step out of your comfort zone into the unknown to have what you have stated you want for your life. There is a difference between having a *hunger* and having *desire.*

Hunger makes you want to nibble. It is a willingness to step into the shallow water without committing to go any further. It is really governed by fear and uncertainty.

Hunger looks for others to go in front and do it for you. You will come, but only after they have forged the trail and cleared the jungle. You want them to do the work and you share in the rewards. If it doesn't work, you have someone or something to blame and an excuse to walk away without anything being your fault.

Desire is different. It is inner strength that believes you can achieve this. It is an internal calmness about what *is*, that is demonstrated with an outer focus and determination. The excitement of the moment has been replaced with the enthusiasm about the journey. It is your mind, being fed through your imagination, creating possibilities. It is your imagination unleashed and free to explore the world of options. It is you, facing your fears and having a desire that can see through the darkness the fear uses. It is you, driven by the need to know *who* you really are and *what* you can really achieve.

When you can answer these three questions, your dream is alive and filled with the energy necessary to take you forward into the real world of personal success. When the answers are clear in your mind and supported with your emotions, there is no stopping you; there are no limitations on what you can achieve.

Just remember — these are not one time questions. These are the questions you will need to ask each time the journey redesigns itself or a new journey is presented to you. These are the guiding questions of life.

Dreams are sketches; you will not always achieve them in the form you have planned. They may look different when you get there.

Dreams are possibilities that need shape and color. This can only be achieved through action and behavior.

Dreams contain freedom. That is why your imagination has so much fun with them. Your mind knows that without a dream you are trapped in repeating, and lack the energy to explore. Exploring is where life was meant to be lived.

Here are some questions for you to *honestly* answer:

- *What do you really want for your life?*

- *Why do you really want it?*

- *What price are you really willing to pay to achieve it?*

What Does A Dream Offer Your Life?

D *direction*

R *realizations*

E *energy with a purpose*

A *a sense of purpose*

M *mission, ministry, crusade*

You and the Others
In Your Life

*The behavior of others in your life is consistent
with your design for their lives.*

Have you ever wondered why some people
want to be in charge, and then, when things go
wrong, don't want to be held accountable? I see it
in the lives of people every day.

I see it with parents and their children. They
wonder what has happened to their children. They
didn't raise them to be the way they are. They
don't understand what has happened. Granted,
there are some "bad" children, but most children
are simply living out what their parents have told
them is okay. When you look at the behavior of
children, you are seeing their definition of
parenting.

They want to plan their own life, *but* when
things don't go the way they wanted them to go, it
wasn't their fault. They just had a run of bad luck.
Now, they expect you to bail them out. Hear me
say this! Don't bail them out. If you do, you have
now made them dependent on you. They must face
what they have done and work their way through
to the other side.

171

If you know the rules
and break them,
you must
pay the
consequences.

I see it in marriages that go in the wrong
direction. It wasn't their fault. The other person
just wouldn't work with them. Now, divorce
becomes their way of justifying what didn't work.
The tragedy is that if they don't work through this
one, it will more than likely repeat itself again in
the next relationship. You cannot move beyond the
lessons you are not willing to learn.

I see it in business. Business drops off, and
those at the top want to blame those on the front
line. They are not working hard enough! The
economy has gotten soft. They want to look at
everyone, except themselves.

One day I received a phone call from a
gentleman I had met at a conference where I was
speaking in Kansas City. My topic was *Building A
Partnership With Your People.* I talked about some
of the companies I had worked with to redesign the
internal workings of the company. I will never
forget the conversation.

"Richard, I was at your program in Kansas
City. I must tell you I was captivated by what you
were talking about."

"Thanks, Chuck. When you are able to
create that partnership, most of the little things that
drive you crazy just go away."

"I have been thinking long and hard about what you said. What would it take for you to come to my company and get my people straight?"

"Interesting choice of words Chuck. Let's see if I heard what you said. What would it take for me to come to your company and get your people straight? Is that what you said?"

"Yeah! I have got a problem with my people and I need your help in getting them moving in the right direction."

"Chuck, where do you fit into this equation?"

"Oh, I know what needs to be done. I just need your help in convincing my people that I am right."

He didn't get it! *The behavior of others in your life is consistent with your design for their lives.* They are what you have designed them to be. When you look at them, you are seeing what your presence has told them is okay behavior.

My all-time favorite happened a few years ago in Las Vegas. I was there to address a very large international convention. I was staying at the Las Vegas Hilton. I got up, got ready and started my journey to the convention center. I was through the casino and was making a left turn when I almost ran into this gentleman.

He paused, looked at me and said, "You're Richard Flint!"

"Yes, I am."

"I can't believe this. I can't believe I am standing this close to you. Man, I really believe in what you say. I have many of your tapes and videos. I play them for my people all the time."

He paused, caught his breath and continued. "You are the reason I am here. I got the program information, saw your name and made the decision to come. I even brought most of my people. They are in the room waiting to listen to you. I want to tear them up."

I said, "Thank you. Are you going to be at the presentation?"

The look on his face changed and this was his reply. "No, I don't need that crap!"

He didn't get it! Any improvement in his people would have to be led by his presence. The behavior of all those people in his work environment is consistent with the design he has for them. Since you cannot lead another person past the point where you are, if you are not growing, what do you have to offer them?

You really do define the presence of others in your life. Have you ever been guilty of giving someone a second chance for the sixth time? Do they ever keep repeating the same behavior over and over? Have you ever wondered *why* they do that?

The answer is really simple. You have told them that it is okay! Once they know you are not going to do anything, they feel it is okay to do what they want. It is not their issue; they are simply doing what you have given them permission to do.

It is like:

• a parent telling a child "you do that again and you are going to be punished." The child tests with the same behavior and there is not a consequence to what they did. What does the child believe?

• a parent telling a teenager "I expect you home by 11:00 P.M." The teenager comes in at 1:00 A.M. and there is not a consequence to what they did. What does the teenager believe?

• a company having a Policy and Procedure Manual that explains company behavior. A person goes against the policy and leadership doesn't do anything. What message has leadership just sent to the people?

FACT: Most people are going to test you to see if you mean what you say.

Why? Why would they do that?

Because most have been brought up in a world of inconsistencies. Words have been uttered, tested and found to be just words. Too many have gotten through life by testing the rules and not being held accountable for their behavior. When they know there is no consequences to what they do, they feel they have permission to repeat it. If they test the rules and get punished with a consequence that doesn't fit the crime, they feel the lack of seriousness commitment. Again, they look at the result and feel it must be okay to continue to do what they want to do.

The reality is that we have become a nation of people who don't understand the need to hold people accountable for their behavior. Much of the violence, crime and lack of respect for life is the direct result of not holding people accountable for their behavior. It starts in the lack of a home life and continues throughout the life of a person.

We have become a nation where too many people are willing to justify, rather than step up and make a person accountable for their behavior. The reality should be that if you break the rules, you pay the consequences.

What ever happened to parents who would spank their child? I am not talking about beating their children. That is not an option here. I'm talking about a swat on the rear end that called attention to what they had done.

What is wrong with getting a child's attention? What's all this stuff about not wanting to "harm" the child's psyche? My dad spanked me. I knew if I broke the rules, there were going to be consequences. Don't you know, that made me stop and think about what I was going to do.

If there are rules and the child breaks the rules, there should be consequences that get their attention. If the rules can be broken without the proper consequences, there are no rules.

What's wrong with discipline? What's the issue with holding a person accountable for their behavior? People need to know the rules; they need to know if they break the rules, there will be consequences.

Without rules that hold people accountable, ugly people will just get uglier. Without rules that hold people accountable, people have no respect for others. Without rules that hold people accountable, right and wrong hold very little meaning. Without rules that hold people accountable, all behavior becomes acceptable.

A society that justifies itself and doesn't hold people accountable for what they do, is a self destructive society. Look around! Doesn't that seem to be the direction where we have been and where we are headed?

Here are some questions for you to *honestly* answer:

- *Should you be held accountable for your behavior?*

- *Do you think we have become a nation that is too soft?*

- *Do you let people get by with breaking your rules?*

Why Do People Need To Be Held Accountable?

H *have no place to hide*

E *expectations are clearly in place*

L *lets them know the rules*

D *defines and holds to consequences*

Notes

YOUR #1 CHALLENGE

Your biggest challenge is getting beyond all your old emotional negative tapes.

Leslie was one of the most talented people I ever met, but lived in a world of "I can't." I met him via the telephone. His brother had been in one of my programs and had recommended that Leslie give me a call.

When he called he connected with Hilda. Now, if you have ever called my office and heard this little southern voice answer the phone, that is Hilda. Hilda can charm anyone. I had this man call in one day to return an audio album, which he had two of, and before he got off the phone, he had purchased three other albums. He told me, "All I intended on doing was returning the duplicate album, and before I knew it, I was ordering your three new albums."

That is Hilda!

Leslie had a ton of questions about me. Hilda answered each of them and told him I would give him a call. It couldn't have been ten minutes later that I called the office and Hilda give me his name, number and run down on him. When I called, he was surprised.

You become the emotional tapes you listen to. If those tapes are negative, you become negative. If they are positive, you become positive. They are your design for living.

Later, Leslie told me, "I didn't expect you to call me back. I figured that lady I talked to thought I was crazy and would never give you the message."

That was Leslie. He lived in a world where everything was right with others, but nothing was right with him. *Yet*, when you met him, you quickly realized this was one of the most brilliant people you have ever met. He just couldn't see it. His world was one where he compared himself to others and always made sure he came out on the short end of the stick.

Leslie's childhood instilled this in him. His family was very affluent and his mom and dad were both very intelligent. Their expectations for him and his brother were very high. His brother was very outgoing and excelled at everything he did. When his parents would talk to Leslie about him, Leslie was always the "inferior" one. He was never as smart as, never as outgoing as, never as perfect as his brother.

Leslie told me during one of our visits "There was never a conversation between my parents and me that I wasn't compared to him. I felt like I was a major disappointment to them. Richard, I would try to please them, but they always found something wrong with what I had done. It was so difficult living in his shadow. There were days I wished my brother would die."

The tragedy occurred when Leslie was in his early teens. His brother died. It was the most devastating thing that had ever happened in his life. Leslie put it this way. "I thought I had killed my brother. I had wished he would die, and he did. I made the mistake of telling my parents what I had wished, and I became the enemy. They couldn't believe I had done that."

There was this long pause during this conversation, and the tears began to flow. "That has haunted me for years. I have several pictures of us together, and each time I look at one of them, I break down."

Can you imagine what that did to Leslie emotionally? It created an emotional tape that he could not get rid of.

Once life began to settle down again, his parents raised the stakes for Leslie. Now, he was not only expected to be perfect, but to be everything they had planned for his brother. Leslie put it this way: "Life became a living hell. Every day was a day of torture and punishment. My life was under the microscope and every day got torn apart. I couldn't do anything right."

While in college, he met Sarah. Sarah was beautiful, smart and the person he wanted to marry. It wasn't long after they married that Leslie realized he had married into a family just like his.

Sarah's father was a person who lived in a world that was either black or white. There was no room for interpretation. He was always right, and you didn't question anything he said. The two daughters had grown up revering their father. He was a god in their eyes. Leslie was accepted because of Sarah, but was never really allowed inside the family. He was just there, like it had been with his family.

Sarah's business became very successful. Her fame and reputation grew. Every time Leslie turned around, she was receiving another plaque or being honored by this and that group. Leslie existed in her world. He worked in "her" company taking care of all her computer needs.

You see, when it came to computers and technology, Leslie was a genius. He wrote program after program for her company. The programs were so far advanced that it made Sarah's company the leader in the field. Much of the recognition she received was because of the technology Leslie had created. Much of their company's success was because of the technology that Leslie designed. Yet, when Sarah was interviewed or accepted her awards, Leslie was never mentioned. He was the shadow who got to tag along and stand beside his wife.

Each day Leslie felt like he was becoming less and less of a person. Put yourself in his position:

- You're married to a very successful person who lets you know it is her success.
- You work for your spouse and she lets you know it is her company.
- You work to build her company through your expertise, and you are never recognized as part of the success.
- When you go to her family gatherings, you are the outsider who is not involved in the family conversations and is made to feel like a stranger.

Put yourself in Leslie's place; *how would you feel?*

When Leslie and I started our growth journey together, he had just been asked by a major publisher to write a book on data modules. At one of the computer shows he had attended, he met a gentleman who realized the special gift Leslie had been given. Their conversations had led to this gentleman putting the publishing company in contact with Leslie. This should have been one of the most exciting times in his life, *but* it had become one of the most depressing.

When he shared the publisher's request with Sarah, she made fun of it. Her words were "That is just going to be a waste of time. We have more important things to do around here. The company is growing and I need you focused on our needs here, not some foolish book. Besides, you never finish what you start anyway. It will be just another waste."

Our first meeting was a very emotional meeting. When I work with my private coaching people, our first meeting involves me doing a historical journey of their life from birth until the present. When we first started the conversation, Leslie was very quiet.

I said, "Leslie, I cannot help you if you don't share with me. You are not going to tell me anything I haven't heard from others. You are not going to tell me anything that is going to shock me or make me think less of you. I am here to guide you and I need you to honestly share information with me. I am your friend, not someone looking to hurt you."

Well, that is all it took for him to open his life and his emotional vault. All those years of living in the shadow of his brother came pouring out. All the pressure of never being good enough in his parents' eyes came gushing out. The years of living in Sarah's shadow and feeling like an outsider in all aspects of her life were now flowing through his emotional filters.

Here was this talented and very gifted young man, controlled by the environments that had made him feel unloved, unworthy and unwanted. His life was a series of negative tapes that just kept playing in his head. Each and every time something good would happen in his life, the "Old" Leslie would turn it into a negative and emotionally beat him with it.

Leslie shared with me some of the thoughts he was wrestling with, concerning writing the book.

- *"I don't really have anything to offer."*
- *"It would never sell."*
- *"I could never write it; I am not a writer."*
- *"It would just be another failure in my life."*

These were all old tapes that had been recorded from his childhood. I wish people understood the power of the messages we get from childhood. In my working with human behavior, so many of the struggles people deal with as adults come from the messages they were given as a child. Childhood is where you discover who you are, gain a sense of what you can do, and it programs you with the messages you will carry with you into adulthood. You become the emotional tapes you listen to. If those tapes are negative, you become negative. If they are positive, you become positive. They are your design for living.

Your #1 challenge in life is to let go of the negative tapes and rerecord them with positive information. You cannot erase them, *but* you can edit them. It is not easy; it is filled with fear; it means getting honest with yourself; it means facing those people who keep throwing the negative at you. It is the most challenging journey you will ever undertake.

It took us fifteen months to get Leslie positioned to move forward. It meant facing some tough issues. He had to confront his parents; he had to confront Sarah's parents; he had to confront Sarah. None of these were easy. Each one took an emotional toll on Leslie, *but* on the other side the emotional toll, it was worth it.

I wish you could see Leslie today. If you had

seen him before and now, you would not recognize him. His first book became a trendsetter for the world of data modeling. It is used by most of all the top computer companies in North America. His second book has followed the same success trail as the first. He has become a highly requested speaker at technology conventions.

What happened to Leslie? The same thing that needs to happen to so many. He faced the "Old" Leslie and took away his control. Every day, individuals make the choice to either continue in the Circle of Sameness, which is controlled by the "Old" You, or face the "Old" You and free the "New" You to direct your life.

This internal battle for control of your life is a war. The "Old" You uses all the old negative tapes to create worry, doubt and uncertainty. Each is designed to keep you trapped in the world of sameness. Each weapon the "Old" You uses has been created to hold you an emotional hostage.

The "New" You wants you to be free from the Circle of Sameness. The "New" You wants you to sense, feel and taste life. The "New" You wants you to live in today preparing for an even better tomorrow.

This is a war! The "Old" You knows if the

"New" You wins, he is no longer in control of your life. Make no mistake; this battle is being fought for control of your life. The winner gets to design who you are, what you can be and what you can achieve.

Here are some questions for you to *honestly* answer:

- *Do you have internal battles between your desires and your fears?*

- *Do you find yourself frustrated with what is not happening in your life?*

- *Do you get tired of wrestling with the same issues?*

What Does It Take For The "New" You To Win The Battle?

B *believe in yourself*

A *address the "Old" You out loud*

T *trust in your talents*

T *tackle the issues one at a time*

L *live through your desire, not your fear*

E *expect things to just get better and better*

191

Notes

YOU ARE NEVER ALONE

YOU ARE NEVER ALONE

I am a spiritual person.

How do you know what you are supposed to do with your life? You have several ideas, and all of them sound okay. How do you know what is the right thing for you to do?

I have taught for years that God created the human race and wants them to have three things:

- *Happiness*
- *Personal Fulfillment*
- *Freedom*

This has become the gauge I use to know what is right and wrong for my life. If where I am does not offer me the possibility to achieve these three, then it is not the right place for my life. These three working with me are what will bring my life a sense of purpose, the feeling of completion and will allow me to be the very best I can be.

It is tragic, but so many spend their time on this earth trying to find happiness. They look to things; they depend on others; they run from place to place. In the end, they live with disappointment and a feeling that they are lost.

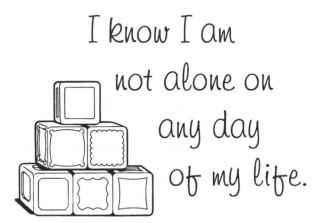

I know I am
not alone on
any day
of my life.

Things can only create moments. Once you obtain the "thing," it will never be enough. Now you have to have the next best "thing." Their lives become endless circles with the rooms filled with all the "things" that never made them happy. Then, each time they look at them, it just feeds their feeling of emptiness.

People cannot give you happiness, personal fulfillment or freedom. Oh, they can create moments where you think you can have them, *but* if they can give them to you, they can also take them away. It becomes a game where "If you do what I want you to do, I will reward you with the feeling of love. If you don't, I will take it away from you." This creates an environment based on *need*, not true love and respect.

So, what do they do when things and people cannot give them a sense of what life is about? They pack up mentally and emotionally (and sometimes physically) and run to the new pasture that looks green. When they get there, it doesn't take long to repeat their needy behaviors and once again experience their empty feeling.

It makes their lives a soap opera. There are very few, if any, *WOW* moments they can use to celebrate life. They don't seem to attract people who enjoy them and in turn enjoy having that person in their life. They bring people in who play with their emptiness and use them to fulfill their own personal needs. When it is no fun, or you are no longer willing to play by their rules, they cast you aside and move on to their next victim.

Time on this earth is really short. Life is about being able to celebrate the gift of life. Life is about finding your personal value and sharing it with others. Through sharing it with others you are made better; you become smarter; you stand taller. The purpose of life is for you to be able to stand in front of the mirror, look at yourself and be able to say *I love who I am because I am a person who, through the grace of God, is alive and living.*

In 1978 my life had reached a place where I wasn't experiencing the joy of my day; I didn't end the day feeling fulfilled; I was feeling trapped and no longer in control of my life.

I was working with St. Paul Title Insurance Company in the Palm Beaches. My role was to create a presence for the company through doing counseling for salespeople and programs for companies. Three years prior, when I had started, there could have been no job better suited for where I was in my growth journey. It gave me the opportunity to use my gift of taking people beyond their personal confusion.

God in His wisdom has given me a gift that for a long time I saw as a curse and a blessing. The gift is the unique ability to show people the pathway through the jungle of their life. I can help people find the resolution to the confusion that is draining their lives of its positive energy.

In the beginning of learning about my gift, I saw this as a curse. I could stand in the midst of a life and have a clear picture of what was going on without them saying a word to me. It made people very uncomfortable being around me. They felt it, I felt it and if they didn't want to face their life, they would run as fast as their little legs would carry them.

It was a great blessing, because if you wanted to improve your life by facing those issues that were holding you hostage, I could show you the pathway to resolution. My great joy was watching people find the real meaning to happiness, personal fulfillment and freedom. It was seeing them break free of their Circle of Sameness and discover the meaning of inner success.

In '78 I was really searching for the next great adventure for my life. I believed that God had brought me to St. Paul Title to show me there was life after being on the church staff. Some things had happened there that left me with a sour taste in my life. Part of me had wanted to give up on believing there was good in people. Every person has an ugly side and — pushed enough — that ugly side can rule their lives. Most of us never get pushed that far. We may have negative times, but we don't let the ugly out.

Well, I have been part of a situation where the ugly was out, not just in one person, *but* in an entire group of people. They were on a seek-and-destroy mission. If you were on their "hit list," you were going to be destroyed. I was on that list. I withstood them as long as possible, but finally decided to leave.

When I left, I wasn't sure what I was going to do. Homer Duval was President of St. Paul in the Palm Beaches. He approached me about helping him build the presence of the company in Palm Beach County. The idea he presented would allow me to use my talents and remove me from the uglies.

Homer told me one time "I don't know why I ever approached you with this idea. It was not something I had been planning for a long time. It was just something that felt right."

Well, I knew why he approached me. Homer was a very spiritual person who lived seeking to do God's will for his life. His coming to me was not his doing.

After two years of working with St. Paul there was this nagging feeling that my time there was complete. I just didn't know where to go or what to do.

One of my options was to take my speaking talent and branch out into the world of public speaking. My time with St. Paul had opened many doors with companies and local Real Estate Associations. Each time I would do one program, I would get requests from several others. It was great exposure for the company, and Homer would always tell me to go do them. So, I would go, speak and get more requests.

I thought this would be fun, but I was really nervous about doing this on my own. What happens if I cannot build this into a business? There must be something that isn't as risky. In reality this was just an old tape from my mother that was playing in my head. She had always told me "You will never amount to anything in life. You will always be a failure."

I had worked hard to prove her wrong, *but* every now and then, that old tape would turn on and create doubt. I just wasn't sure what to do.

Years before, while I was at Southwestern Theological Seminary, I had a class in the

"Meaning of Prayer." One of the discussions we had was how to use prayer as a discovery tool. I had always used prayer as a time of conversation with God, thanking Him for life, asking His guidance as I worked with people and bringing my concern about others to Him. I had not really thought about using prayer to ask God for a sign.

Dr. Roy Fish was my professor and on this day we were talking about Fleece Praying. Dr. Fish said, "There are times in your life when you are going to be confused and uncertain about life. You are going to feel lost and fearful of making the wrong decision. At that time ask God for a sign."

I had never forgotten that lecture, nor had I ever really done it. Alone one morning in my personal quiet time, I was really struggling with the feeling I was going through. I enjoyed the role I had at St. Paul, yet I knew it was coming to an end. I was nervous, scared and filled with questions about what all this meant. I decided to put Dr. Fish's lesson to the test.

I said, "God, I need your help. I know you brought me to St. Paul, but I also know my mission here is almost over. I believe You have a plan for my life that will continue to allow me to use my gifts, *but* I don't know what it is. Show me with a sign that will leave no doubt about my journey."

I finished my quiet time, got ready and headed to my office. When I walked in, my assistant was talking on the phone. She paused, looked at me and said, "There is a Nancy Schultz on the phone from Gallery of Homes who would like to talk to you."

I looked at her and thought, "I don't know any Nancy Schultz."

I was familiar with Gallery of Homes. They were one of the premier real estate franchises in North America.

I said, "Okay, put her through."

I walked into my office, picked up the phone and began a conversation with Nancy Schultz.

"Richard, I know you don't know me and I don't know you, *but* several of our brokers in the Palm Beaches told me to call you. We are having our national convention at Innisbrook right outside Tampa, and I was wondering if you would do a session for us?"

My silence must have lasted for an hour. Finally, she said, "Are you there?"

"Yes, I am here. Nancy, I am not sure. I have done a lot of local programs, but have never spoken for a national convention before."

"Richard," she continued. "My brokers in the Palm Beaches tell me you are very good and have a lot to teach us. We will cover your expenses and pay you $1,500 to do a 90 minute breakout session for us."

$1,500! No one had ever paid me before. I did programs as a part of my job with St. Paul. Before I realized what I was saying I said, "Okay."

"Great. We will look forward to having you at our convention."

I hung up the phone, paused and whispered to God "Is this Your doing? How do I know this is the answer I was looking for?"

For the next few weeks I wrestled with whether this was the sign I was looking for. I had so many questions about this being the answer to my quest.

Three weeks from the day Nancy had called, I walk into my office and my assistant is talking on the phone. She pauses, looks at me and says, "It's Nancy Schultz and she needs to talk to you."

I go into my office, pick up the phone and say "Hello" to Nancy.

"Richard, I need your help" were her opening words. "I have just lost one of my Keynote speakers and am in a bind to replace him. We are going to press with our final program and I have to fill his spot. I was talking to the chairman of the convention committee, Mary Harker, and

she suggested I ask you. She told me about this
talk you do on dreaming. Would you do it for us?"

My heart was racing. Doing a breakout
session for a few people was much different than
speaking for a few thousand people. Sure, I had
filled the pulpit at First Baptist when Dr. Moody
was out of town, but that was church — not a
convention.

"Nancy," I said. "I am not sure. I was okay
with the breakout session, but doing a keynote in
front of the entire group. I need to think about
this."

"I understand, *but* I need your answer within
the next hour."

Something inside me spoke up. It wasn't
me, but this voice from inside said "Okay, I will do
it."

I hung up the phone, took a deep breath and
muttered, "Okay God, if you are trying to show
me, I think I get the picture."

In that moment I was semi-calm with the
idea that my future was going to be speaking. After
all, it was my strength.

Three months went by, and the time of the
Gallery of Homes convention arrived. I was
driving across the state and was having all these
doubts play with me again. God and I were

talking. Well, I was talking and I was hoping God was listening.

I said, "God, I want to be really sure before I make this move. I think You are leading me in this, but I have got to be certain about this. This is my future we are talking about. So, can I ask for one more sign? If this is the right thing for me to do, show me through the response of the people to what I do."

Now, I was the opening speaker at the convention. When I arrived in the ballroom, it was packed. The ceremonies began and it was time for me to speak. I had 45 minutes to talk about "Living Your Dream." I was nervous and scared. I took a deep breath and delivered my insights. After the opening session came the first of my three breakouts.

Oh, I forget to tell you, Nancy had called back and added two more breakout sessions to my schedule. Each time she called this little voice inside me just said "Yes!"

As I approached my room, I noticed this crowd of people. It was still 35 minutes until I was to speak. What were they doing here? I stepped into the room and it was packed. There was not a chair to be found, there was no space on the floor to sit and before we started there were people standing on chairs out in the hall so they could see in.

Each of the other two sessions were more packed than the first. They moved me to a larger room for the third session and it was just as crowded.

I've got to tell you, when I finished that day, I was exhausted, but on an emotional high. I went to my room, opened the curtains, stared at the heavens and said, "Okay God, I get the message. I know what Your plan is for my life. Thanks for being consistently persistent with me."

From that day until now I have never questioned the direction of my life. I know what my mission in life is. I know that what I do is my ministry. I understand God gave me the gift of helping people find the clarity in the midst of their confusion. I sense and accept the responsibility that goes with it. I know I am not alone in any aspect of my life.

Each speaking day I look at the meeting room and God and I talk. Well, I talk and He listens. I say, "You have made this possible. I place my life in Your hands to be used to show people the pathway to removing the confusion, the pain and the frustration from their lives. Use me to make a difference in their lives."

I am a spiritual person. I know I am not alone on any day of my life. The hand of God directs me; the Word of God calms me; the opportunities to speak keep me focused on my need to challenge myself to keep growing in my understanding and clarity. I am a spiritual person who doesn't have to face any part of life alone.

Here are some questions to *honestly* answer:

- *Are you happy fulfilled and free in your life?*

- *Are you where you should be in your life?*

- *Do you listen to your spiritual nature?*

How Do You Know When You Are In The Right Place?

R *respond to, do not react to, the uneasy moments*

I *inwardly, there is a sense of peace*

G *growth is still happening*

H *handling the moments of doubt is easy*

T *there is this feeling of purpose inside you*

206

BUILDING BLOCKS
Life is a choice you make each day through the decisions you implement.

Every now and then I watch some of the high profile TV talk shows and listen to people expound on their pain, the injustices of life and what others have done to complicate or destroy their life. I think "Don't they get it! Their lives are the result of the choices they have made."

It is not about whether life is fair or not. That is not the issue. Life is a *result*. It is the result of the choices you make. If you choose to do dumb things, you will get the results that go with that behavior. If you choose to do the right things, you get the results that go with that decision.

It is not about what pain you have experienced. Pain is a result, and can either cause you to put the healing process in place or repeat the behaviors that have created the pain in the first place.

Life is not about the injustices your life has been handed. Every life is handed challenges that they can either work through or allow to become problems that they drag with them from day to day.

If you choose to live your life avoiding the "what is" of life, then you get to travel a journey

Without consequences, rules have no meaning.

that reaps those rewards. You are perfectly designed to achieve what you are achieving.

If you choose to face the "what is" in life, you get to move forward with energy designed to show you the possibilities that life was designed to offer you. You are perfectly designed to achieve what you are achieving.

Fred King was one of the closest people I have ever had in my life. We met through Sales and Marketing International. Someone had given Fred an audio copy of the presentation at their international convention. He was so interested in the material that he contacted my office to talk to me. That conversation started a friendship that grew stronger and stronger.

He was this 6'2" gentleman who had a presence that could captivate people. He was soft spoken, but filled with wisdom that was worth listening to. The one thing you learned about Fred was *don't play games with him.* He was an on-the-table, in-your-face person who wouldn't let problems arise.

Fred and Sharon were constantly meeting us somewhere to either play golf or take in the sounds of New York City. When the four of us were together, Karen and Sharon were always off shopping, and Fred and I would be solving the challenges of the world.

One weekend the four of us were at the Doral Golf Resort & Spa in Miami for a long weekend. The ladies were doing their thing at the spa and Fred and I were doing our thing on the golf course. Fred had just finished his sales reviews with his sales force and was a chatter box.

He was the District Manager for Blue Cross and Blue Shield of Alabama. I have spoken for his salespeople and was familiar with the challenges he was having with the group. He had been asked to build the group with a lot of very young people. He had a few seasoned salespeople, but the majority were in their mid-to-late twenties.

We were waiting to tee off on the first tee when a conversation began that lasted the entire round. He was very concerned because of some of the things his sales reviews had presented him with.

"These are interesting days we are living in," was his opening. "These young people seem to be so lost. It is as if they are walking around in a fog. They want it all, *but* they don't want to really work to get it. They expect things to be given to them and then just reap the rewards."

"Fred, so many have grown up in homes that taught them to be irresponsible, rather than accountable for their behavior. If they get into trouble, mom and dad are there to bail them out. If they need something, mom and dad are there to get it for them. They have a limited understanding of what it means to be self-sufficient."

"I have some young sales people who don't have a clue what it means to work. They show up each day anticipating that things are going to be done for them. When you talk to them about expectation, they look at you like you are speaking a foreign language. You cannot talk to them about having a dream; they have no comprehension of what that means. They just want to make a lot of money so they can have their toys and the lifestyle they were handed growing up."

There was this long pause followed by this look of concern. "Richard, they just don't have a solid foundation to build their life on. That's the real issue. They live on shifting sand and don't seem to understand the need for a solid foundation."

Fred's words were so true. Over the years, as I have invested my life, my time, my insights in people, I have marveled at how many live on the shifting sand. Each day is filled with crisis from the sand shifting. Each day they struggle to hold themselves together. Each day they search to find something or someone to lean on. Each day they fall deeper into the pit of blame, reason and justification. Because they live on shifting sand, it is challenging for them to understand the need for a solid foundation. Because they have mastered the art of blame, they feel no sense of responsibility for what they are wrestling with in life. They simply look for someone to bail them out.

Too many times they can run back to mom and dad and they will protect them from their upside-down world. Recently, I was talking to a couple who are being challenged by their 17-year-old daughter. She is their third child and so different from her older sisters. Linda and Joel are really wrestling with what to do. One part says "protect her and don't be too tough on her. After all, she is still a child."

On the other hand, another part says "She has to be responsible for her behavior. If there are no consequences to what she does, she will never learn the realities of life."

They asked me for help. My philosophy of behavior has not weakened over the years. I think there should always be consequences to wrong behavior. If one is always protected from the results of their negative choices, they will just keep repeating them. If they are held accountable and not bailed out, they learn they have to be responsible for what they do.

My words to them were simple. "Let her fall down. Stop protecting her from her negative behaviors. If you are always there to catch her, she will never feel the pain or experience the consequences of her negative behavior. Besides, she knows you will always be there to protect her, so what's the big deal about doing what she wants to do? Mom and dad won't let her get hurt."

Does that sound tough? I have had people tell me for years "If you love someone, you protect them."

I don't agree with that. If you love someone, your love doesn't protect them from facing their wrongs. It holds them accountable for their behavior. Protecting them from facing their wrongs only gives them permission to do it again. Only when you know there are consequences, will you think about what you are going to do. Isn't this the real challenge with the justice system in our country? Hey, it doesn't matter what you do. You can find a reason and a way to get by with it. Without consequences, rules have no meaning.

We need to get back to instilling in people Building Blocks. We need to show people how to move from living on shifting sand to building their

213

lives on a solid foundation of principles. When principles disappear, anything is okay. When one doesn't have to be accountable for one's behavior, laws mean very little. When a person can live without respecting the rights of others, society becomes its own enemy.

Bottom line: life is a series of choices you make. With each choice there are behaviors. Those behaviors define what that life can or cannot be. There is no one to blame; there is no escaping personal accountability. If a person chooses the journey, they must accept the results of their choices. Until that is the rule of life, we will continue as a society without a solid foundation.

But, when we return to understanding the need for those Building Blocks, we can begin to redesign ourselves as a people of principles, ethics, truth, trust, accountability and love. It cannot happen without the Building Blocks.

Notes

Other books by Richard Flint, CSP:

The Reality of Stress

Breaking Free

Life Is A Maze

Quiet Please

Feelings

It Takes A Lot Of Pain To Grow Up

Reflections

Sometimes I Really Need To Cry